JUNIOR GREAT BOOKS

SERIES 2

SECOND SEMESTER

◆ ◆ ◆

AN INTERPRETIVE READING, WRITING,

AND DISCUSSION CURRICULUM

JUNIOR GREAT BOOKS

SERIES 2

SECOND SEMESTER

THE GREAT BOOKS FOUNDATION

A nonprofit educational corporation

15 14 13 12 11

Printed in the United States of America

Published and distributed by

THE GREAT BOOKS FOUNDATION

A nonprofit educational corporation

35 East Wacker Drive, Suite 2300

Chicago, IL 60601-2298

Contents

He caught sight of a fine red balloon.

THE RED BALLOON

Albert Lamorisse

Once upon a time in Paris there
lived a little boy whose name was Pascal.
He had no brothers or sisters, and he
was very sad and lonely at home.

Once he brought home a lost cat, and
some time later a stray puppy. But his
mother said animals brought dirt into the
house, and so Pascal was soon alone
again in his mother's clean well-kept
rooms.

Then one day, on his way to school,
he caught sight of a fine red balloon,

tied to a street lamp. Pascal laid his schoolbag on the ground. He climbed up the lamppost, untied the balloon, and ran off with it to the bus stop.

But the conductor knew the rules. "No dogs," he said. "No large packages, no balloons."

People with dogs walk. People with packages take taxis.

People with balloons leave them behind.

Pascal did not want to leave his balloon behind, so the conductor rang the signal bell and the bus went on without him.

Pascal's school was a long way off, and when he finally reached the school door it was already shut. To be late for school and with a balloon—that was unheard of! Pascal was very worried.

Then he had an idea. He left his balloon with the janitor, who was sweeping the yard. And since it was the first time that he had ever been late, he was not punished.

When school was over, the janitor, who had kept the balloon in his room for Pascal, gave it back to him.

...

But it had begun to rain. And Pascal had to walk home because of those silly rules about balloons on buses. But he thought his balloon shouldn't get wet.

There was an old gentleman just going by, and Pascal asked him whether he and the balloon could take shelter under his umbrella. So, from one umbrella to another, Pascal made his way home.

Why is Pascal so worried about getting his balloon wet?

His mother was
glad to see him
finally come home.
But since she had been
very worried, she was
angry when she found out
that it was a balloon that had
made Pascal late. She took the
balloon, opened the window,
and threw it out.

Now, usually when you let a
balloon go, it flies away. But Pascal's
balloon stayed outside the window,
and the two of them looked at each
other through the glass. Pascal was
surprised that his balloon hadn't flown
away, but not really as surprised as
all that. Friends will do all kinds of things
for you. If the friend happens to be a
balloon, it doesn't fly away. So Pascal
opened his window quietly, took his
balloon back inside, and hid it in
his room.

The next day, before he left for school, Pascal opened the window to let his balloon out and told it to come to him when he called.

Then he picked up his schoolbag, kissed his mother goodbye, and went downstairs.

When he reached the street he called: "Balloon! Balloon!" and the balloon came flying down to him.

Then it began to follow Pascal—without being led by a string, just as if it were a dog following its master.

But, like a dog, it didn't always do as it was told. When Pascal tried to catch it to cross the street, the balloon flew beyond his reach.

Pascal decided to pretend he didn't care. He walked up the street

just as if the balloon weren't there at all
and hid behind the corner of a house.
The balloon got worried and hurried
to catch up with him.

When they got to the bus stop, Pascal
said to the balloon: "Now, balloon, you
follow me. Don't lose sight of the bus!"

That was how the strangest sight came
to be seen in a Paris street—a balloon
flying along behind a bus.

When they reached Pascal's school,
the balloon again tried not to let itself be
caught. But the bell was already ringing
and the door was just about to close,
so Pascal had to hurry in alone. He was
very worried.

But the balloon flew over the school
wall and got in line behind the children.
The teacher was very surprised to see this
strange new pupil, and when the balloon
tried to follow them into the classroom,
the children made so much noise that the
principal came along to see what was
happening.

*Why does the
balloon want
to follow the
children into
the classroom?*

15

The principal tried to catch the balloon to put it out the door. But he couldn't. So he took Pascal by the hand and marched him out of school. The balloon left the classroom and followed them.

The principal had urgent business at the Town Hall, and he didn't know what to do with Pascal and his balloon. So he locked the boy up inside his office. The balloon, he said to himself, would stay outside the door.

But that wasn't the balloon's idea at all. When it saw that the principal had put the key in his pocket, it sailed along behind him as he walked down the street.

All the people knew the principal very well, and when they saw him walking past followed by a balloon they shook their heads and said: "The principal's

playing a joke. It isn't right; a principal should be dignified, he shouldn't be playing like one of the boys in his school."

The poor man tried very hard to catch the balloon, but he couldn't, so there was nothing for him to do but put up with it. Outside the Town Hall the balloon stopped. It waited for him in the street, and when the principal went back to school the balloon was still behind him.

The principal was only too glad to let Pascal out of his office and to be rid of him and his balloon.

•••

On the way home Pascal stopped to look at a picture in a sidewalk exhibit. It showed a little girl with a hoop. Pascal thought how nice it would be to have a friend like that little girl.

But just at that moment he met a real little girl, looking just like the one in the picture. She was wearing a pretty white dress, and she held in her hand the string . . . to a blue balloon!

Pascal wanted to be sure she noticed that his balloon was a magic one. But his balloon wouldn't be caught, and the little girl began to laugh.

Pascal was angry. "What's the use of having a trained balloon if it won't do what you want?" he said to himself. At that very moment some of the tough boys of the neighborhood came by. They tried to catch the balloon as it trailed along behind Pascal. But the balloon saw the danger. It flew to Pascal at once.

He caught it and began to run, but more boys came to corner him from the other side.

So Pascal let go of his balloon, which immediately rose high into the sky. While the boys were all looking up, Pascal ran between them to the top of the steps. From there he called his balloon, which came to him at once— to the great surprise of the boys in the gang.

So Pascal and his balloon got home without being caught.

Why does keeping the balloon give Pascal so many worries? (Underline two or three things on this page that help you answer this question.)

The next day was Sunday. Before he left for church, Pascal told his balloon to stay quietly at home, not to break anything, and especially not to go out. But the balloon did exactly as it pleased. Pascal and his mother were hardly seated in church when the balloon appeared and hung quietly in the air behind them.

Now, a church is no place for a balloon. Everyone was looking at it and no one was paying attention to the service. Pascal had to leave in a hurry, followed out by the church guard. His balloon certainly had no sense of what was proper. Pascal had plenty of worries!

All this worry had made him hungry. And as he still had his coin for the collection plate, he went into a bakeshop for some cake. Before he went inside he said to the balloon: "Now be good and wait for me. Don't go away."

•••

The balloon was good, and only went as far as the corner of the shop to warm itself in the sun. But that was already too far. For the gang of boys who had tried to catch it the day before saw it, and they thought that this was the moment to try again. Without being seen they crept up to it, jumped on it, and carried it away.

When Pascal came out of the bakeshop, there was no balloon! He ran in every direction, looking up at the sky. The balloon had disobeyed him again!

It had gone off by itself! And although he called at the top of his voice, the balloon did not come back.

The gang had tied the balloon to a strong string, and they were trying to teach it tricks. "We could show this magic balloon in a circus," one of them said. He shook a stick at the balloon. "Come here or I'll burst you," he shouted.

As luck would have it, Pascal saw the balloon over the top of a wall, desperately dragging at the end of its heavy string. He called to it.

•••

As soon as it heard his voice, the balloon flew toward him. Pascal quickly untied the string and ran off with his balloon as fast as he could run.

The boys raced after them. They made so much noise that everyone in the neighborhood stopped to watch the chase. It seemed as if Pascal had stolen the boys' balloon. Pascal thought: "I'll hide in the crowd." But a red balloon can be seen anywhere, even in a crowd.

Pascal ran through narrow alleys, trying to lose the gang of boys.

At one point the boys didn't know whether Pascal had turned right or left, so they split up into several groups. For a minute Pascal thought he had escaped them, and he looked around for a place to rest. But as he rounded a corner he bumped right into one of the gang. He ran back the way he had come, but there were more boys there. He was desperate—he ran up a side street which led to an empty lot. He thought he'd be safe there.

But suddenly boys appeared from every direction, and Pascal was surrounded.

So he let go of his balloon. But this time, instead of chasing the balloon, the gang attacked Pascal. The balloon flew a little way off, but when it saw Pascal fighting it came back. The boys began throwing stones at the balloon.

"Fly away, balloon! Fly away!" Pascal cried. But the balloon would not leave its friend.

Then one of the stones hit the balloon, and it burst.

While Pascal was crying over his dead balloon, the strangest thing happened!

Everywhere balloons could be seen flying up into the air and forming a line high into the sky.

It was the revolt of all captive balloons!

And all the balloons of Paris came down to Pascal, dancing around him, twisting their strings into one strong one and lifting him up into the sky. And that was how Pascal took a wonderful trip all around the world.

"Everything's nicer on the other side of the hill."

The Other Side of the Hill

Elizabeth Coatsworth

There was once a sizable pine tree that stood a little by itself in a hilly pasture. Its shade made a fine place for the cows and sheep to rest when they grew tired of eating grass in the sun, and its branches were well shaped for building nests. The rabbits, too, stopped in its shelter on their way to the farmer's garden; and the squirrels raced up and down its trunk and flung themselves gaily from branch to branch. Altogether, the pine tree had a good deal of company and heard a good deal of talk.

One day a rabbit came hop-hop-hopping and stopped in its special corner between two roots.

"Where have you been, rabbit?" asked the tree politely.

"I've just been over the hill to the next farm," said the rabbit. "It's wonderful. Their lettuces are much finer than the ones on our farm. Their house is larger; their weather vane is brighter.

Everything's much nicer on the other side of the hill."

"I've always thought ours was a very fine farm," said the pine tree a little stiffly.

Soon after that a bird settled in its branches.

"Where do you come from, stranger?" asked the pine tree with its usual politeness.

"I come from the north:
Southward I fly—
Over the hill
And into the sky!
Over the hill
And far away
To a starrier night
And a brighter day!"

sang the bird, who, like other birds, always talked in poetry.

"I think very well of our own climate," said the pine tree uneasily.

Soon a sheep came to lie in the shade, staring out straight before her with her eyes like marbles.

"What are you thinking about, sheep?"
asked the pine tree.

"I'm thinking how good the grass looks
on the other side of the hill," said the
sheep, "and I'm wondering if the fence
is too tight for me to get through it."

"I do wish you could talk about
something except the other side of the
hill!" cried the pine tree crossly. "Don't
you know that I can't even look over?
It's mean for all you creatures who have
feet and wings to keep talking about
things I'll never see!"

"Hoity-toity!" said the sheep, rising. "What a temper you're in, to be sure! You nearly made me swallow my cud. I'll rest in some shade where I can have peace, thank you."

And the sheep walked off offended. The tree wanted to apologize, but it didn't exactly know what it had done that was so wrong. And, anyway, the sheep was soon out of hearing. The pine tree was left alone. Or was it alone?

A voice nearby was remarking:

"So you'd like to go to the other side of the hill, would you?"

It wasn't the voice of bird, beast, insect, or creeping thing. The pine tree looked about with surprise. Then it saw who had spoken. It was a gnome sitting on a rock, under a parasol made of glistening pine needles with small cones at the end of the ribs. The gnome was eating blueberries from a large leaf shaped like a bowl.

"So you'd like to go to the other side of the hill, would you?" he repeated, taking another mouthful. "Well, why don't you?"

"Because trees can't move," said the pine tree. "I wish you wouldn't make fun of me, gnome."

"You never know what you can do till you try," said the gnome. "Try."

The pine tree tried.

Something among its roots seemed to stir and move; something pushed against the earth; something lifted up the pine tree; something carried it away from the spot where it had spent all its life since it was a seed.

"Oh! Oh! I'm falling!" the pine tree cried in terror.

"You're walking," said the gnome coolly. "I've given you legs. Now, try to keep your balance better. It takes practice of course."

By the end of the afternoon the pine tree could walk nicely.

The first place it went to was a pool in which to see itself.

"I do look rather funny," the pine tree giggled.

It *did* look rather funny.

Why doesn't the pine tree mind that it looks funny?

Above was the sizable pine tree, with
its trunk and wide green branches—an
unusually handsome tree. Then came
a fringe of roots, gathered up neatly like
a petticoat; and then came two sturdy
brown legs that looked ready to caper.

The tree went back to the gnome,
who was still perched on the rock.

"Well, you're off!" said the gnome.
"Have a good time. I'll see you when you
come back."

"I don't believe I'll ever come back,"
said the tree.

"We'll see," said the gnome and waved
as the pine tree started off to the top of
the hill.

The first thing that the wandering tree
met was a cow grazing peacefully in the
late afternoon light with a jingle-jangle
bell at her neck.

"Hello," said the pine politely.

The cow looked up, saw the pine tree
moving toward her on its stout brown
legs, uttered a moo of wild terror,

flung up her tail,
and bounded off down
the pasture at a speed that
would curdle her milk for a week.

The tree paid no attention to her but
looked abroad over the landscape. There
was the big farm the rabbit had told
about, the bright weather vane, the green
lettuces. And beyond these there were
distant villages, white church spires,
and farther hills with a road winding
across them.

"Ah, I must see everything," thought the
tree, turning to seek the road. First it
climbed a wall or two, with a little trouble.

Then, when
it finally reached the road,
it felt so happy and eager to
see things that it started to run.
It ran on and on, very well pleased with
itself. A horse in a nearby meadow
looked up, gave a neigh of terror, and
galloped off along the wall. The pine tree
put on speed and beat the horse to the
end of the pasture.

"Of course," it said to the horse, who
was panting, "I had better footing than
you did. But I'd have beaten you anyhow
if we'd both been on the road, I think.
Can't you jump the wall, and we'll have a
little race as far as the railroad track?"

*Why does the
pine tree
want to have
another race
with the horse?*

36

"I don't want to!"
gasped the horse. "I don't want
to come anywhere near you! Go away!"

"Oh, because I have legs, I suppose,"
said the pine tree airily. "Well, you have
four of them yourself, but I'm not
afraid of *you*!"

Leaving the horse to think about this
remark, the tree continued on its way. It
walked rather jauntily till it heard a small,

angry voice remark from the hole high up in its trunk:

"Will you please stop jiggling my babies?"

It was the mother squirrel. The tree had quite forgotten about her. It had remembered that the birds' nests were empty now, but it hadn't thought about squirrels.

"I'm sorry," it said, slowing down to a less jouncy walk.

"That's better," remarked the squirrel. "I have no objection to travel if it's comfortable. My children have reached an age when it should broaden their minds. But no jouncing, *if* you please. And when you stop, see that we're near an oak tree, so we can have a bite to eat."

The pine tree agreed politely. It wasn't sure whether it was pleasant to have company or not. It decided it wasn't.

Those young squirrels were practically full grown now. They didn't need a nest, the tree decided.

It stopped near an oak.

"There's your supper, squirrels," it called genially.

The squirrels clambered down its trunk and into the oak, where they were soon merrily cracking acorns. The tree looked hard at the oak. Sure enough, there was a good hole in its trunk that didn't seem to be occupied. The squirrels could use it, or they could walk home.

"So long!" called the pine, suddenly making off down the road as fast as it could go.

It heard an angry scurry behind it but paid no attention. It ran on for a mile or so and then stopped. There was no further pursuit.

"It's not an adventure if there are too many others along," thought the pine tree, settling down to a comfortable walk.

For days the pine tree traveled far and wide. It saw many strange things and creatures, and astonished most of those that it saw. But at last it began to long for home and its own hillside and the creatures it had always known.

Once the pine tree began to be homesick, it was very homesick indeed.

Why does the pine tree begin to be homesick?

•••

One night, as it was resting with its feet in a little brook, it woke up and suddenly thought, "Why shouldn't I start home this very minute?" And start home it did.

It ran all through the moon-dappled night. It ran all through the rosy dawn. It ran all through the bright morning. And just before noon it reached its own hillside, climbed the two walls and with a contented sigh settled itself to rest. But this time it took a position a little higher up in the pasture, so that, any time it cared to, it might look over the hill at the next-door farm and the road and the villages beyond.

Everyone made a great fuss over the tree's return. There were so many rabbits and birds and sheep about that it seemed like a regular party.

The gnome came, still under his parasol, and said, "So you're back?" in a friendly way, and never added, "I thought you would be."

The cow came, too, and said, "If you ever have the notion to going off again, warn me first. I wasn't myself for a week, but I dunno as I blame you for wanting to go."

The squirrel came with her family and settled again in the old hole.

"You were mean to go off without us!" she declared. "We had to walk all the way home. But it's something to be able to say that we live in the only tree that ever went traveling, so I intend to forget what you did to us and say no more about it."

From that day on the pine tree never left the pasture again. It was quite content, for now it could see the other side of the hill. And if the birds and animals talked about their adventures, the tree had its own adventures to talk about,

much more interesting than any of theirs.
Sometimes, when asked, it would sing
for them its own song:

"Oh, any bird can fly,
 can fly,
And any sheep can run;
But it's only a tree, a
 traveling tree,
That really can have fun!
For everything it sees,
 it sees,
Is new as new can be;
And everyone shouts out,
 very loud,
Hi! look at the traveling tree!"

"The Emperor is in his wardrobe!"

THE EMPEROR'S NEW CLOTHES

Hans Christian Andersen

Many years ago there lived an Emperor who was so exceedingly fond of fine new clothes that he spent all his money on being elaborately dressed. He took no interest in his soldiers, no interest in the theater, nor did he care to drive about in his state coach, unless it were to show off his new clothes. He had different robes for every hour of the day, and just as one says of a King that he is in his Council Chamber, people always said of him, "The Emperor is in his wardrobe!"

The great city in which he lived was
full of gaiety. Strangers were always
coming and going. One day two
swindlers arrived. They made themselves
out to be weavers and said they knew
how to weave the most magnificent
fabric that one could imagine. Not only
were the colors and patterns unusually
beautiful, but the clothes that were made

of this material had
the extraordinary
quality of becoming
invisible to everyone
who was either
unfit for his post or
inexcusably stupid.

"What useful clothes to
have!" thought the Emperor.
"If I had some like that, I might
find out which of the people in
my Empire are unfit for their posts.
I should also be able to distinguish
the wise from the fools. Yes, that material
must be woven for me immediately!"
Then he gave the swindlers large sums
of money so that they could start
work at once.

Quickly they set up two looms and
pretended to weave, but there was
no trace of anything on the frames.
They made no bones about demanding
the finest silk and the purest gold
thread. They stuffed everything into

their bags and continued to work at the empty looms until late into the night.

"I'm rather anxious to know how much of the material is finished," thought the Emperor, but to tell the truth, he felt a bit uneasy, remembering that anyone who was either a fool or unfit for his post would never be able to see it. He rather imagined that he need not have any fear for himself, yet he thought it wise to send someone else first to see how things

•••

were going. Everyone in the town knew about the exceptional powers of the material, and all were eager to know how incompetent or how stupid their neighbors might be.

"I will send my honest old Chamberlain to the weavers," thought the Emperor. "He will be able to judge the fabric better than anyone else, for he has brains, and nobody fills his post better than he does."

So the nice old Chamberlain went into the hall where the two swindlers were sitting working at the empty looms.

"Upon my life!" he thought, opening his eyes very wide, "I can't see anything at all!" But he didn't say so.

Do you think the Emperor is being wise or foolish when he decides to send someone else to see the material first? Why?

•••

Both the swindlers begged him to be good enough to come nearer, and asked how he liked the unusual design and the splendid colors. They pointed to the empty looms, and the poor old Chamberlain opened his eyes wider and wider, but he could see nothing, for there was nothing. "Heavens above!" he thought, "could it possibly be that I am stupid? I have never thought that of myself, and not a soul must know it. Could it be that I am not fit for my post? It will never do for me to admit that I can't see the material!"

"Well, you don't say what you think of it," said one of the weavers.

"Oh, it's delightful—most exquisite!" said the old Chamberlain, looking through his spectacles. "What a wonderful design and what beautiful colors! I shall certainly tell the Emperor that I am enchanted with it."

"We're very pleased to hear that," said the two weavers, and they started

describing the colors and the curious
pattern. The old Chamberlain listened
carefully in order to repeat, when he
came home to the Emperor, exactly what
he had heard, and he did so.

The swindlers now demanded more
money, as well as more silk and gold
thread, saying that they needed it for
weaving. They put everything into their

pockets and not a thread appeared upon the looms, but they kept on working at the empty frames as before.

Soon after this, the Emperor sent another nice official to see how the weaving was getting on and to inquire whether the stuff would soon be ready. Exactly the same thing happened to him as to the Chamberlain. He looked and looked, but as there was nothing to be seen except the empty looms, he could see nothing.

"Isn't it a beautiful piece of material?" said the swindlers, showing and describing the pattern that did not exist at all.

"Stupid I certainly am not," thought the official. "Then I must be unfit for my excellent post, I suppose. That seems rather funny—but I'll take great care that nobody gets wind of it." Then he praised the material he could not see and assured them of his enthusiasm for the gorgeous colors and the beautiful pattern.

•••

"It's simply enchanting!" he said to the
Emperor.

The whole town was talking about
the splendid material.

Why is the Emperor so easily fooled by the swindlers? (Underline two or three things on these pages that help you answer this question.)

•••

And now the Emperor was curious to see it for himself while it was still upon the looms.

Accompanied by a great number of selected people, among whom were the two nice old officials who had already been there, the Emperor went forth to visit the two wily swindlers. They were now weaving madly, yet without a single thread upon the looms.

"Isn't it magnificent?" said the two nice officials. "Will Your Imperial Majesty deign to look at this splendid pattern and these glorious colors?" Then they pointed to the empty looms, for each thought that the others could probably see the material.

"What on earth can this mean?" thought the Emperor. "I don't see anything! This is terrible. Am I stupid? Am I unfit to be Emperor? That would be the most disastrous thing that could possibly befall me."

...

"Oh, it's perfectly wonderful!" he said. "It quite meets with my Imperial approval." And he nodded appreciatively and stared at the empty looms—he would not admit that he saw nothing. His whole suite looked and looked, but with as little result as the others. Nevertheless, they all said, like the Emperor, "It's perfectly wonderful!" They advised him to have some new clothes made from this splendid stuff and to wear them for the first time in the next great procession.

"Magnificent!" "Excellent!" "Prodigious!" went from mouth to mouth, and everyone was exceedingly pleased. The Emperor gave each of the swindlers a decoration to wear in his buttonhole, and the title of "Knight of the Loom."

Before the procession they worked all
night, burning more than sixteen candles.
People could see how busy they were
finishing the Emperor's new clothes. They
pretended to take the material from the
looms, they slashed the air with great
scissors, they sewed with needles without
any thread, and finally they said, "The
Emperor's clothes are ready!"

Then the Emperor himself arrived with
his most distinguished courtiers, and

each swindler raised an
arm as if he were holding
something and said,
"These are Your
Imperial Majesty's
knee-breeches. This
is Your Imperial
Majesty's robe. This
is Your Imperial
Majesty's mantle,"
and so forth. "It is
all as light as a
spider's web.
One might fancy
one had nothing
on, but that is just
the beauty of it!"

"Yes, indeed," said all the courtiers,
but they could see nothing, for there
was nothing to be seen.

"If Your Imperial Majesty would
graciously consent to take off your
clothes," said the swindlers, "we could
fit on the new ones in front of the
long glass."

···

So the Emperor laid aside his clothes, and the swindlers pretended to hand him, piece by piece, the new ones they were supposed to have made. And they fitted him round the waist and acted as if they were fastening something on—it was the train. And the Emperor turned round and round in front of the long glass.

"How well the new robes suit Your Imperial Majesty! How well they fit!" they all said. "What a splendid design! What gorgeous colors! It's all magnificently regal!"

"The canopy which is to be held over Your Imperial Majesty in the procession is waiting outside," announced the Lord High Chamberlain.

"Well, I suppose I'm ready," said the Emperor. "Don't you think they are a nice fit?" And he looked at himself again in the glass, first on one side and then the other, as if he really were carefully examining his handsome attire.

The courtiers who were to carry the train groped about on the floor with fumbling fingers and pretended to lift it. They walked on, holding their hands up in the air. Nothing would have induced them to admit that they could not see anything.

And so the Emperor set off in the procession under the beautiful canopy, and everybody in the streets and at the windows said, "Oh! how superb the

Emperor's new clothes are! What a
gorgeous train! What a perfect fit!"
No one would acknowledge that he
didn't see anything, so proving that
he was not fit for his post, or that
he was very stupid.

None of the Emperor's
clothes had ever met with
such a success.

"But he hasn't got any clothes on!" gasped out a little child.

"Good heavens! Hark at the little innocent!" said the father, and people whispered to one another what the child had said. "But he hasn't got any clothes on! There's a little child saying he hasn't got any clothes on!"

"But he hasn't got any clothes on!" shouted the whole town at last. The Emperor had a creepy feeling down his spine, because it began to dawn on him that the people were right. "All the same," he thought to himself, "I've got to go through with it as long as the procession lasts."

So he drew himself up and held his head higher than before, and the courtiers held on to the train that wasn't there at all.

Why does the Emperor feel that he must go on with the procession?

61

The unhappiest of all the creatures was Bombo.

HOW THE ELEPHANT BECAME

Ted Hughes

Long ago when the world was
brand new, before animals or birds,
the sun rose into the sky and
brought the first day.

The flowers jumped up and stared
round astonished. Then from every side,
from under leaves and from behind
rocks, creatures began to appear.

In those days the colours were much
better than they are now, much brighter.
And the air sparkled because it had
never been used.

But don't think everything was so easy.

···

To begin with, all the creatures were
pretty much alike—very different from
what they are now. They had no
idea what they were going to
become. Some wanted to
become linnets, some
wanted to become lions,
some wanted to become
other things. The ones
that wanted to become
lions practised at being lions—
and by and by, sure enough, they
began to turn into lions. So, the ones
that wanted to become linnets practised
at being linnets, and slowly they turned
into linnets. And so on.

But there were other creatures
that came about in
other ways. . . .

...

The unhappiest of all the creatures was Bombo. Bombo didn't know what to become. At one time he thought he might make a fairly good horse. At another time he thought that perhaps he was meant to be a kind of bull. But it was no good. Not only the horses, but all the other creatures too, gathered to laugh at him when he tried to be a horse. And when he tried to be a bull, the bulls just walked away shaking their heads.

"Be yourself," they all said.

Bombo sighed. That's all he ever heard: "Be yourself. Be yourself." What was himself? That's what he wanted to know.

So most of the time he just stood, with sad eyes, letting the wind blow his ears this way and that, while the other creatures raced around him and above him, perfecting themselves.

"I'm just stupid," he said to himself. "Just stupid and slow and I shall never become anything."

That was his main trouble, he felt sure.
He was much too slow and clumsy—and
so big! None of the other creatures was
anywhere near so big. He searched hard
to find another creature as big as he was,
but there was not one. This made him
feel all the more silly and in the way.

But this was not all. He had great ears
that flapped and hung, and a long, long
nose. His nose was useful. He could pick
things up with it. But none of the other
creatures had a nose anything like it.
They all had small, neat noses, and they
laughed at his. In fact, with that and his
ears and his long white sticking-out
tusks, he was a sight.

...

As he stood, there was a sudden
thunder of hooves. Bombo looked up
in alarm.

"Aside, aside, aside!" roared a huge
voice. "We're going down to drink."

Bombo managed to force his
way backwards into a painful clump
of thornbushes just in time to let
Buffalo charge past with all his family.
Their long black bodies shone, their
curved horns tossed, their tails
screwed and curled,

as they pounded down towards the water in a cloud of dust. The earth shook under them.

"There's no doubt," said Bombo, "who they are. If only I could be as sure of what I am as Buffalo is of what he is."

Then he pulled himself together.

"To be myself," he said aloud, "I shall have to do something that no other creature does. Lion roars and pounces, and Buffalo charges up and down bellowing. Each of these creatures does something that no other creature does. So. What shall I do?"

He thought hard for a minute.

Then he lay down, rolled over onto his back, and waved his four great legs in the air. After that he stood on

his head and lifted his hind legs
straight up as if he were going to
sunburn the soles of his feet.
From this position, he lowered
himself back onto his four
feet, stood up, and looked
round. The others should
soon get to know me by
that, he thought.

Nobody was in sight,
so he waited until a pack
of wolves appeared on
the horizon. Then he
began again. Onto his
back, his legs in the air,
then onto his head, and his
hind legs straight up.

"Phew!" he grunted, as he lowered
himself. "I shall need some practice
before I can keep this up for long."

When he stood up and looked round
him this second time, he got a shock.
All the animals were round him in a ring,
rolling on their sides with laughter.

"Do it again! Oh, do it again!" they were crying as they rolled and laughed. "Do it again. Oh, I shall die with laughter. Oh, my sides, my sides!"

Bombo stared at them in horror.

After a few minutes the laughter died down.

"Come on!" roared Lion. "Do it again and make us laugh. You look so silly when you do it."

But Bombo just stood. This was much worse than imitating some other animal. He had never made them laugh so much before.

He sat down and pretended to be inspecting one of his feet, as if he were alone. And, one by one, now that there was nothing to laugh at, the other animals walked away, still chuckling over what they had seen.

"Next show same time tomorrow!" shouted Fox, and they all burst out laughing again.

Bombo sat, playing with his foot, letting the tears trickle down his long nose.

Well, he'd had enough. He'd tried to be himself, and all the animals had laughed at him.

That night he waded out to a small island in the middle of the great river that ran through the forest. And there,

from then on, Bombo
lived alone, seen by nobody
but the little birds and a
few beetles.

One night, many years later,
Parrot suddenly screamed and
flew up into the air above the
trees. All his feathers were singed.
The forest was on fire.

Within a few minutes, the animals
were running for their lives. Jaguar,
Wolf, Stag, Cow, Bear, Sheep, Cockerel,
Mouse, Giraffe—all were running side
by side and jumping over each other
to get away from the flames.
Behind them, the fire came
through the treetops
like a terrific
red wind.

...

"Oh dear! Oh dear! Our houses, our children!" cried the animals.

Lion and Buffalo were running along with the rest.

"The fire will go as far as the forest goes, and the forest goes on forever," they cried, and ran with sparks falling into their hair. On and on they ran, hour after hour, and all they could hear was the thunder of the fire at their tails.

On into the middle of the next day, and still they were running.

At last they came to the wide, deep, swift river. They could go no farther. Behind them the fire boomed as it leapt from tree to tree. Smoke lay so thickly over the forest and the river that the sun could not be seen. The animals floundered in the shallows at the river's edge, trampling the banks to mud, treading on each other,

coughing and sneezing in the white
ashes that were falling thicker than thick
snow out of the cloud of smoke. Fox sat
on Sheep and Sheep sat on Rhinoceros.

They all set up a terrible roaring,
wailing, crying, howling, moaning sound.
It seemed like the end of the animals.
The fire came nearer, bending over them
like a thundering roof, while the black
river swirled and rumbled beside them.

Out on his island stood Bombo,
admiring the fire which made a fine sight
through the smoke with its high spikes
of red flame. He knew he was
quite safe on his island.
The fire couldn't cross
that great stretch of
water very easily.

At first he didn't see the animals
crowding low by the edge of the water.
The smoke and ash were too thick
in the air. But soon he heard them.
He recognized Lion's voice shouting:

"Keep ducking yourselves in the water.
Keep your fur wet and the sparks will
not burn you."

And the voice of Sheep crying:

"If we duck ourselves we're swept
away by the river."

And the other creatures—Gnu, Ferret,
Cobra, Partridge, crying:

"We must drown or burn. Goodbye,
brothers and sisters!"

It certainly did seem like the end of
the animals.

Without a
pause, Bombo pushed
his way into the water.
The river was deep, the current
heavy and fierce, but Bombo's
legs were both long and strong.
Burnt trees, that had fallen into the
river higher up and were drifting
down, banged against him,
but he hardly felt them.

Why does Bombo rush to save the other animals "without a pause"?

76

In a few minutes he was coming up into shallow water towards the animals. He was almost too late. The flames were forcing them, step by step, into the river, where the current was snatching them away.

Lion was sitting on Buffalo, Wolf was sitting on Lion, Wildcat on Wolf, Badger on Wildcat, Cockerel on Badger, Rat on Cockerel, Weasel on Rat, Lizard on Weasel, Tree-Creeper on Lizard, Harvest Mouse on Tree-Creeper, Beetle on Harvest Mouse, Wasp on Beetle, and on top of Wasp, Ant, gazing at the raging flames through his spectacles and covering his ears from the roar.

∙∙∙

When the animals saw Bombo
looming through the smoke, a great shout
went up:

"It's Bombo! It's Bombo!"

All the animals took up the cry:

"Bombo! Bombo!"

Bombo kept coming closer. As he
came, he sucked up water in his long
silly nose and squirted it over his back to
protect himself from the heat and the
sparks. Then, with the same long, silly
nose he reached out and began to pick
up the animals, one by one, and seat
them on his back.

"Take us!" cried Mole.

"Take us!" cried Monkey.

He loaded his back with the creatures
that had hooves and big feet; then he
told the little clinging things to cling onto
the great folds of his ears. Soon he had
every single creature aboard. Then he
turned and began to wade back across
the river, carrying all the animals of
the forest towards safety.

Once they were safe on the island
they danced for joy. Then they sat down
to watch the fire. Suddenly Mouse gave
a shout:

"Look! The wind is bringing sparks
across the river. The sparks are blowing
into the island trees. We shall burn
here too."

···

As he spoke, one of the trees on the edge of the island crackled into flames. The animals set up a great cry and began to run in all directions.

"Help! Help! Help! We shall burn here too!"

But Bombo was ready. He put those long silly tusks of his that he had once been so ashamed of under the roots of the burning tree and heaved it into the river. He threw every tree into the river till the island was bare. The sparks now fell onto the bare torn ground where the animals trod them out easily. Bombo had saved them again.

Next morning the fire had died out at the river's edge. The animals on the island looked across at the smoking, blackened plain where the forest had been. Then they looked round for Bombo.

He was nowhere to be seen.

"Bombo!" they shouted. "Bombo!" And listened to the echo.

But he had gone.

He is still very hard to find. Though he is huge and strong, he is very quiet.

But what did become of him in the end? Where is he now?

Ask any of the animals, and they will tell you:

"Though he is shy, he is the strongest, the cleverest, and the kindest of all the animals. He can carry anything and he can push anything down. He can pick you up in his nose and wave you in the air. We would make him our king if we could get him to wear a crown."

According to the story, is being yourself something you need to practice, or does it come naturally?

In the country of Ashanti . . .

ANANSI'S FISHING EXPEDITION

West African folktale as told by
Harold Courlander and George Herzog

In the country of Ashanti, not far from the edge of the great West African forest, there was a man named Anansi, who was known to all the people for miles around. Anansi was not a great hunter, or a great worker, or a great warrior. His specialty was being clever. He liked to outwit people. He liked to live well, and to have other people do things for him. But because all the people of the country knew about Anansi and had had trouble with him, he had to keep thinking of new ways to get something for nothing.

One day
Anansi was sitting
in the village when a man
named Osansa came along.

"I have an idea," Anansi said.
"Why don't we go and set fish traps
together? Then we shall sell the fish and
be quite rich."

But Osansa knew Anansi's reputation
very well, and so he said:

"No, I have as much food as I can eat
or sell. I am rich enough. Why don't
you set your fish traps by yourself?"

"Ha! Fish alone? Then I'd have to do
all the work!" Anansi said. "What I need
is a fool for a partner."

Osansa went away, and after a while another man named Anene came along.

"I have an idea," Anansi said. "Why don't the two of us go and set fish traps together? Then we shall sell the fish and be quite rich."

Anene knew Anansi very well too, but he seemed to listen thoughtfully.

"That sounds like a fine idea," he said. "Two people can catch more fish than one. Yes, I'll do it."

The news went rapidly around the village that Anansi and Anene were going on a fishing expedition together. Osansa met Anene in the market and said:

"We hear you are going to trap fish with Anansi. Don't you know he is trying to make a fool of you? He has told everyone that he needs a fool to go fishing with him. He wants someone to set the fish traps and do all the work, while he gets all the money for the fish."

"Don't worry, friend Osansa, I won't be Anansi's fool," Anene said.

Why is Anene able to trick Anansi here? (Underline one or two things on these pages that help you answer this question.)

❧

•••

Early the next morning Anansi and Anene went into the woods to cut palm branches to make their fish traps.

Anansi was busy thinking how he could make Anene do most of the work. But when they came to the place where the palm trees grew, Anene said to Anansi:

"Give me the knife, Anansi. I shall cut the branches for the traps. We are partners. We share everything. My part of the work will be to cut branches, your part of the work will be to get tired for me."

"Just a minute, let me think," Anansi said. "Why should I be the one to get tired?"

86

"Well, when there's work to be done someone must get tired," Anene said. "That's the way it is. So if I cut the branches the least you can do is to get tired for me."

"Hah, you take me for a fool?" Anansi said. "Give me the knife. I shall cut the branches and *you* get tired for *me*!"

So Anansi took the knife and began cutting the branches from the trees. Every time he chopped, Anene grunted. Anene sat down in the shade and groaned from weariness, while Anansi chopped and hacked and sweated. Finally the wood for the fish traps was cut. Anansi tied it up into a big bundle. Anene got up from the ground holding his back and moaning.

"Anansi, let me carry the bundle of wood now, and you can get tired for me," Anene said.

"Oh, no, my friend Anene," Anansi said, "I am not that simpleminded. I'll carry the wood myself, and you can take the weariness for me."

So he hoisted the bundle to the top of his head and the two of them started back to the village. Anene groaned all the way.

"Oh, oh!" he moaned. "Take it easy, Anansi! Oh, oh!"

When they came to the village Anene said:

"Let me make the fish traps, Anansi, and you just sit down and get tired for me."

"Oh, no," Anansi said. "You just keep on as you are." And he made the fish traps while Anene lay on his back in the shade with his eyes closed, moaning and groaning.

And while he was making the traps,
working in the heat with perspiration
running down his face and chest, Anansi
looked at Anene lying there taking all his
weariness and sore muscles for him,
and he shook his head and clucked
his tongue.

"Anene thinks he is intelligent," he said
to himself. "Yet look at him moaning and
groaning there, practically dying from
weariness!"

When the fish traps were done Anene
climbed to his feet and said, "Anansi, my
friend, now let me carry the fish traps to
the water, and you can get tired for me."

...

"Oh, no," Anansi said. "You just come along and do your share. I'll do the carrying, you do the getting-tired."

So they went down to the water, Anansi carrying and Anene moaning. When they arrived, Anene said to Anansi:

"Now wait a minute, Anansi, we ought to think things over here. There are sharks in this water. Someone is apt to get hurt. So let me go in and set the traps, and should a shark bite me, then you can die for me."

"Wah!" Anansi howled. "Listen to that! What do you take me for? I'll go in the water and set the traps myself, and if I am bitten, then *you* can die for *me*!" So he took the fish traps out into the water and set them, and then the two of them went back to the village.

The next morning when they went down to inspect the traps they found just four fish. Anene spoke first.

"Anansi, there are only four fish here. You take them. Tomorrow there will probably be more, and then I'll take my turn."

"Now, what do you take me for?" Anansi said indignantly. "Do you think I am simpleminded? Oh, no, Anene, you take the four fish and I'll take my turn tomorrow."

So Anene took the four fish and carried them to town and sold them.

Next day when they came down to the fish traps, Anene said:

"Look, there are only eight fish here. I'm glad it's your turn, because tomorrow there doubtless will be more."

"Just a minute," Anansi said. "You want me to take today's fish so that tomorrow you get a bigger catch? Oh no, these are all yours, partner, tomorrow I'll take my share."

So Anene took the eight fish and carried them to town and sold them.

Next day when they came to look in the traps they found sixteen fish.

"Anansi," Anene said, "take the sixteen fish. Little ones, too. I'll take my turn tomorrow."

"Of course you'll take your turn tomorrow, it's my turn today," Anansi said. He stopped to think. "Well, now, you are trying to make a fool out of me again! You want me to take these sixteen miserable little fish so that you can get the big catch tomorrow, don't you? Well, it's a good thing I'm alert! You take the sixteen today and I'll take the big catch tomorrow!"

So Anene carried the sixteen fish to the market and sold them.

Next day they came to the traps
and took the fish out. But by this time
the traps had rotted in the water.

"Well, it's certainly your turn today,"
Anene said. "And I'm very glad of that.
Look, the fish traps are rotten and worn
out. We can't use them any more. I'll tell
you what—you take the fish to town
and sell them, and I'll take the rotten
fish traps and sell them. The fish traps
will bring an excellent price. What a
wonderful idea!"

"Hm," Anansi said. "Just a moment,
don't be in such a hurry. I'll take the fish
traps and sell them myself. If there's such
a good price to be had, why shouldn't
I get it instead of you? Oh, no, *you*
take the fish, my friend."

*Why does
Anansi believe
he will be able
to sell rotten
fish traps for a
lot of money?*

94

Anansi hoisted the rotten fish traps up on his head and started off for town. Anene followed him, carrying the fish. When they arrived in the town Anene sold his fish in the market, while Anansi walked back and forth singing loudly:

"I am selling rotten fish traps! I am selling wonderful rotten fish traps!"

But no one wanted rotten fish traps, and the townspeople were angry that Anansi thought they were so stupid they would buy them. All day long Anansi wandered through the town singing:

"Get your rotten fish traps here! I am selling wonderful rotten fish traps!"

Finally the head man of the town heard about the affair. He too became very angry, and he sent messengers for Anansi. When they brought Anansi to him he asked indignantly:

"What do you think you are doing, anyway? What kind of nonsense is this you are trying to put over the people of the town?"

"I'm selling rotten fish traps," Anansi said, "very excellent rotten fish traps."

"Now what do you take us for?" the chief of the town said. "Do you think we are ignorant people? Your friend Anene came and sold good fish, which the people want, but you come trying to sell something that isn't good for anything and just smell the town up with your rotten fish traps. It's an outrage. You insult us."

The head man turned to the townspeople who stood nearby, listening.

"Take him away and whip him," he said.

The men took Anansi out to the town gate and beat him with sticks. Anansi shouted and yelled and made a great noise. When at last they turned him loose, Anene said to him:

"Anansi, this ought to be a lesson to you. You wanted a fool to go fishing with you, but you didn't have to look so hard to find one. You were a fool yourself."

Anansi nodded his head.

"Yes," he said thoughtfully, rubbing his back and his legs where they had beat him. And he looked reproachfully at Anene. "But what kind of partner are you? At least you could have taken the pain while I took the beating."

Why does Anansi tell Anene, "At least you could have taken the pain while I took the beating"?

The Rabbit was quite the best of all.

THE VELVETEEN RABBIT

Margery Williams

There was once a velveteen rabbit, and in the beginning he was really splendid. He was fat and bunchy, as a rabbit should be; his coat was spotted brown and white, he had real thread whiskers, and his ears were lined with pink sateen. On Christmas morning, when he sat wedged in the top of the Boy's stocking, with a sprig of holly between his paws, the effect was charming.

There were other things in the stocking, nuts and oranges and a toy engine, and chocolate almonds and a clockwork mouse, but the Rabbit was quite the best of all. For at least two hours the Boy loved him, and then Aunts and Uncles came to dinner, and there was a great rustling of tissue paper and unwrapping of parcels, and in the excitement of looking at all the new presents the Velveteen Rabbit was forgotten.

For a long time he lived in the toy cupboard or on the nursery floor, and no one thought very much about him. He was naturally shy, and being only made of velveteen, some of the more expensive toys quite snubbed him. The mechanical toys were very superior, and looked down upon everyone else; they were full of modern ideas, and pretended they were real. The model boat, who had lived through two seasons and lost most of his paint, caught the tone from them and never missed an opportunity of referring to his rigging in technical terms. The Rabbit could not claim to be a model of anything, for he didn't know that real rabbits existed; he thought they were all stuffed with sawdust like himself, and he understood that sawdust was quite out-of-date and should never be mentioned in modern circles. Even Timothy, the jointed wooden lion, who was made by the disabled soldiers and should have had broader views, put on airs and pretended he was connected with Government.

Between them all the poor little Rabbit was made to feel himself very insignificant and commonplace, and the only person who was kind to him at all was the Skin Horse.

•••

The Skin Horse had lived longer in
the nursery than any of the others.
He was so old that his brown coat was
bald in patches and showed the seams
underneath, and most of the hairs in his
tail had been pulled out to string bead
necklaces. He was wise, for he had seen a
long succession of mechanical toys arrive
to boast and swagger, and by-and-by
break their mainsprings and pass away,
and he knew that they were only toys and
would never turn into anything else.
For nursery magic is very strange and
wonderful, and only those playthings that
are old and wise and experienced like
the Skin Horse understand all about it.

"What is REAL?" asked the Rabbit one
day, when they were lying side by side
near the nursery fender, before Nana
came to tidy the room. "Does it mean
having things that buzz inside you and
a stick-out handle?"

"Real isn't how you are made," said the
Skin Horse. "It's a thing that happens

to you. When a child loves you for a long, long time, not just to play with, but REALLY loves you, then you become Real."

"Does it hurt?" asked the Rabbit.

"Sometimes," said the Skin Horse, for he was always truthful. "When you are Real you don't mind being hurt."

"Does it happen all at once, like being wound up," he asked, "or bit by bit?"

"It doesn't happen all at once," said the Skin Horse. "You become. It takes a long time. That's why it doesn't often happen to people who break easily, or have sharp edges, or who have to be carefully kept. Generally, by the time you are Real, most of your hair has been loved off, and your eyes drop out and you get loose in the joints and very shabby. But these things don't matter at all, because once you are Real you can't be ugly, except to people who don't understand."

"I suppose *you* are Real?" said the Rabbit. And then he wished he had not said it, for he thought the Skin Horse might be sensitive. But the Skin Horse only smiled.

"The Boy's Uncle made me Real," he said. "That was a great many years ago; but once you are Real you can't become unreal again. It lasts for always."

The Rabbit sighed. He thought it would be a long time before this magic called Real happened to him. He longed to become Real, to know what it felt like; and yet the idea of growing shabby and losing his eyes and whiskers was rather sad. He wished that he could become it without these uncomfortable things happening to him.

Why is the Rabbit the only toy who asks, "What is REAL?"

There was a person called Nana who
ruled the nursery. Sometimes she took no
notice of the playthings lying about, and
sometimes, for no reason whatever, she
went swooping about like a great wind
and hustled them away in cupboards.
She called this "tidying up," and
the playthings all hated it, especially
the tin ones. The Rabbit didn't mind
it so much, for wherever he was
thrown he came down soft.

One evening, when the Boy
was going to bed, he couldn't
find the china dog that always
slept with him. Nana was in
a hurry, and it was too much
trouble to hunt for china dogs
at bedtime, so she simply looked
about her, and seeing that the
toy cupboard door stood open,
she made a swoop.

"Here," she said, "take your
old Bunny! He'll do to sleep
with you!" And she dragged

the Rabbit out by one ear and put him into the Boy's arms.

That night, and for many nights after, the Velveteen Rabbit slept in the Boy's bed. At first he found it rather uncomfortable, for the Boy hugged him very tight, and sometimes he rolled over on him, and sometimes he pushed him so far under the pillow that the Rabbit could scarcely breathe. And he missed, too, those long moonlight hours in the nursery, when all the house was silent, and his talks with the Skin Horse.

...

But very soon he grew to like it, for the Boy used to talk to him, and made nice tunnels for him under the bedclothes that he said were like the burrows the real rabbits lived in. And they had splendid games together, in whispers, when Nana had gone away to her supper and left the nightlight burning on the mantelpiece. And when the Boy dropped off to sleep, the Rabbit would snuggle down close under his little warm chin and dream, with the Boy's hands clasped close round him all night long.

And so time went on, and the little Rabbit was very happy—so happy that he never noticed how his beautiful velveteen fur was getting shabbier and shabbier, and his tail coming unsewn, and all the pink rubbed off his nose where the Boy had kissed him.

Spring came, and they had long days in the garden, for wherever the Boy went the Rabbit went too. He had rides in the wheelbarrow, and picnics on the grass,

and lovely fairy huts built for him under the raspberry canes behind the flower border. And once, when the Boy was called away suddenly to go out to tea, the Rabbit was left out on the lawn until long after dusk, and Nana had to come and look for him with the candle because the Boy couldn't go to sleep unless he was there. He was wet through with the dew and quite earthy from diving into the burrows the Boy had made for him in the flower bed, and Nana grumbled as she rubbed him off with a corner of her apron.

"You must have your old Bunny!" she said. "Fancy all that fuss for a toy!"

The Boy sat up in bed and stretched out his hands.

"Give me my Bunny!" he said. "You mustn't say that. He isn't a toy. He's REAL!"

Why does the Boy insist that his Rabbit is Real?

•••

When the little Rabbit heard that,
he was happy, for he knew that what
the Skin Horse had said was true at last.
The nursery magic had happened to him,
and he was a toy no longer. He was Real.
The Boy himself had said it.

That night he was almost too happy to
sleep, and so much love stirred in his little
sawdust heart that it almost burst. And
into his boot-button eyes, that had long
ago lost their polish, there came a look of
wisdom and beauty, so that even Nana
noticed it next morning when she picked
him up and said, "I declare if that old
Bunny hasn't got quite a knowing
expression!"

That was a wonderful Summer!

Near the house where they lived
there was a wood, and in the long June
evenings the Boy liked to go there
after tea to play. He took the Velveteen
Rabbit with him, and before he
wandered off to pick flowers, or play
at brigands among the trees, he always

made the Rabbit a little nest somewhere among the bracken, where he would be quite cozy, for he was a kind-hearted little boy and he liked Bunny to be comfortable. One evening, while the Rabbit was lying there alone, watching the ants that ran to and fro between his velvet paws in the grass, he saw two strange beings creep out of the tall bracken near him.

They were rabbits like himself, but quite furry and brand-new. They must have been very well made, for their seams didn't show at all, and they changed shape in a queer way when they moved; one minute they were long and thin and the next minute fat and bunchy, instead of always staying the same like he did. Their feet padded softly on the ground, and they crept quite close to him, twitching their noses, while the Rabbit stared hard to see which side the clockwork stuck out, for he knew that people who jump generally have something to wind them up. But he couldn't see it. They were evidently a new kind of rabbit altogether.

They stared at him, and the little Rabbit stared back. And all the time their noses twitched.

"Why don't you get up and play with us?" one of them asked.

"I don't feel like it," said the Rabbit, for he didn't want to explain that he had no clockwork.

"Ho!" said the furry rabbit. "It's as easy as anything." And he gave a big hop sideways and stood on his hind legs.

"I don't believe you can!" he said.

"I can!" said the little Rabbit. "I can jump higher than anything!" He meant when the Boy threw him, but of course he didn't want to say so.

"Can you hop on your hind legs?" asked the furry rabbit.

That was a dreadful question, for the Velveteen Rabbit had no hind legs at all! The back of him was made all in one piece, like a pincushion. He sat still in the bracken and hoped that the other rabbits wouldn't notice.

"I don't want to!" he said again.

But the wild rabbits have very sharp eyes. And this one stretched out his neck and looked.

"He hasn't got any hind legs!" he called out. "Fancy a rabbit without any hind legs!" And he began to laugh.

"I have!" cried the little Rabbit. "I have got hind legs! I am sitting on them!"

"Then stretch them out and show me, like this!" said the wild rabbit. And he began to whirl round and dance, till the little Rabbit got quite dizzy.

"I don't like dancing," he said. "I'd rather sit still!"

But all the while he was longing to dance, for a funny new tickly feeling ran through him, and he felt he would give anything in the world to be able to jump about like these rabbits did.

The strange rabbit stopped dancing and came quite close. He came so close this time that his long whiskers brushed the Velveteen Rabbit's ear, and then he wrinkled his nose suddenly and flattened his ears and jumped backwards.

"He doesn't smell right!" he exclaimed. "He isn't a rabbit at all! He isn't real!"

"I *am* Real!" said the little Rabbit. "I am Real! The Boy said so!" And he nearly began to cry.

Just then there was a sound of footsteps, and the Boy ran past near them, and with a stamp of feet and a flash of white tails the two strange rabbits disappeared.

"Come back and play with me!" called the little Rabbit. "Oh, do come back! I *know* I am Real!"

But there was no answer, only the little ants ran to and fro, and the bracken swayed gently where the two strangers had passed. The Velveteen Rabbit was all alone.

"Oh, dear!" he thought. "Why did they run away like that? Why couldn't they stop and talk to me?"

For a long time he lay very still, watching the bracken, and hoping that they would come back. But they never returned, and presently the sun sank lower and the little white moths fluttered out, and the Boy came and carried him home.

Weeks passed, and the little Rabbit grew very old and shabby, but the Boy loved him just as much. He loved him so hard that he loved all his whiskers off, and the pink lining to his ears turned gray, and his brown spots faded. He even began to lose his shape, and he scarcely looked like a rabbit anymore, except to the Boy. To him he was always beautiful, and that was all that the little Rabbit cared about. He didn't mind how he looked to other people, because the nursery magic had made him Real, and when you are Real shabbiness doesn't matter.

Why doesn't shabbiness matter when you are Real?

❧

•••

And then, one day, the Boy was ill.

His face grew very flushed, and he talked in his sleep, and his little body was so hot that it burned the Rabbit when he held him close. Strange people came and went in the nursery, and a light burned all night, and through it all the little Velveteen Rabbit lay there, hidden from sight under the bedclothes, and he never stirred, for he was afraid that if they found him someone might take him away, and he knew that the Boy needed him.

It was a long weary time, for the Boy was too ill to play, and the little Rabbit found it rather dull with nothing to do all day long. But he snuggled down patiently, and looked forward to the time when the Boy should be well again, and they would

go out in the garden amongst the flowers
and the butterflies and play splendid
games in the raspberry thicket like they
used to. All sorts of delightful things he
planned, and while the Boy lay half
asleep he crept up close to the pillow and
whispered them in his ear. And presently
the fever turned, and the Boy got better.
He was able to sit up in bed and look at
picture books, while the little Rabbit
cuddled close at his side. And one day,
they let him get up and dress.

It was a bright, sunny morning, and the
windows stood wide open. They had
carried the Boy out onto the balcony,
wrapped in a shawl, and the little Rabbit
lay tangled up among the bedclothes,
thinking.

The Boy was going to the seaside
tomorrow. Everything was arranged,
and now it only remained to carry out
the doctor's orders. They talked about it
all, while the little Rabbit lay under the
bedclothes, with just his head peeping

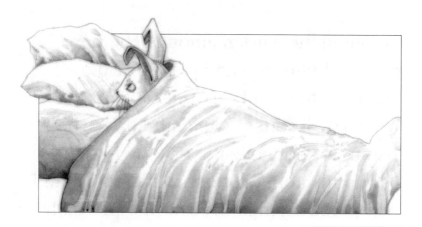

out, and listened. The room was to be disinfected, and all the books and toys that the Boy had played with in bed must be burned.

"Hurrah!" thought the little Rabbit. "Tomorrow we shall go to the seaside!" For the Boy had often talked of the seaside, and he wanted very much to see the big waves coming in, and the tiny crabs, and the sand castles.

Just then Nana caught sight of him.

"How about his old Bunny?" she asked.

"That?" said the doctor. "Why, it's a mass of scarlet fever germs!—Burn it at once. What? Nonsense! Get him a new one. He mustn't have that anymore!"

And so the little Rabbit was put into a
sack with the old picture books and a
lot of rubbish, and carried out to the end
of the garden behind the fowl house.
That was a fine place to make a bonfire,
only the gardener was too busy just then
to attend to it. He had the potatoes to
dig and the green peas to gather,
but next morning he promised
to come quite early and burn the
whole lot.

That night the Boy slept in a
different bedroom, and he had a
new bunny to sleep with him.
It was a splendid bunny, all
white plush with real glass eyes,
but the Boy was too excited to
care very much about it. For
tomorrow he was going to the
seaside, and that in itself was
such a wonderful thing that he
could think of nothing else.

And while the Boy was asleep,
dreaming of the seaside, the little Rabbit

lay among the old picture books in the corner behind the fowl house, and he felt very lonely. The sack had been left untied, and so by wriggling a bit he was able to get his head through the opening and look out. He was shivering a little, for he had always been used to sleeping in a

proper bed, and by this time his coat had worn so thin and threadbare from hugging that it was no longer any protection to him. Nearby he could see the thicket of raspberry canes, growing tall and close like a tropical jungle, in whose shadow he had played with the Boy on bygone mornings. He thought of those long sunlit hours in the garden—how happy they were—and a great sadness came over him. He seemed to see them all pass before him, each more beautiful than the other, the fairy huts in the flower bed, the quiet evenings in the wood when he lay in the bracken and the little ants

ran over his paws; the wonderful day
when he first knew that he was Real.
He thought of the Skin Horse, so wise
and gentle, and all that he had told
him. Of what use was it to be loved and
lose one's beauty and become Real if
it all ended like this? And a tear, a real
tear, trickled down his little shabby
velvet nose and fell to the ground.

And then a strange thing happened. For
where the tear had fallen a flower grew
out of the ground, a mysterious flower,
not at all like any that grew in the
garden. It had slender green leaves
the color of emeralds, and in the
center of the leaves a blossom like
a golden cup. It was so beautiful
that the little Rabbit forgot to cry,
and just lay there watching it. And
presently the blossom opened,
and out of it there stepped a fairy.

She was quite the loveliest fairy
in the whole world. Her dress was
of pearl and dewdrops, and there

were flowers round her neck and in her hair, and her face was like the most perfect flower of all. And she came close to the little Rabbit and gathered him up in her arms and kissed him on his velveteen nose that was all damp from crying.

"Little Rabbit," she said, "don't you know who I am?"

The Rabbit looked up at her, and it seemed to him that he had seen her face before, but he couldn't think where.

"I am the nursery magic Fairy," she said. "I take care of all the playthings that the children have loved. When they are old and worn out and the children don't need them anymore, then I come and take them away with me and turn them into Real."

"Wasn't I Real before?" asked the little Rabbit.

"You were Real to the Boy," the Fairy said, "because he loved you. Now you shall be Real to everyone."

...

And she held the little Rabbit close
in her arms and flew with him into
the wood.

It was light now, for the moon had
risen. All the forest was beautiful, and the
fronds of the bracken shone like frosted
silver. In the open glade between the tree
trunks the wild rabbits danced with their
shadows on the velvet grass, but when
they saw the Fairy they all stopped
dancing and stood round in a ring to
stare at her.

"I've brought you a new playfellow,"
the Fairy said. "You must be very kind to
him and teach him all he needs to know
in Rabbitland, for he is going to live
with you for ever and ever!"

And she kissed the little Rabbit again
and put him down on the grass.

"Run and play, little Rabbit!" she said.

But the little Rabbit sat quite still for a
moment and never moved. For when he
saw all the wild rabbits dancing around
him he suddenly remembered about

his hind legs, and he didn't want them to see that he was made all in one piece. He did not know that when the Fairy kissed him that last time she had changed him altogether. And he might have sat there a long time, too shy to move, if just then something hadn't tickled his nose, and before he thought what he was doing he lifted his hind toe to scratch it.

And he found that he actually had hind legs! Instead of dingy velveteen he had brown fur, soft and shiny, his ears twitched by themselves, and his whiskers were so long that they brushed the grass. He gave one leap and the joy of using those hind legs was so great that he went springing about the turf on them, jumping sideways and whirling round as the others did, and he grew so excited that when at last he did stop to look for the Fairy she had gone.

He was a Real Rabbit at last, at home with the other rabbits.

Autumn passed and Winter, and in the Spring, when the days grew warm and sunny, the Boy went out to play in the wood behind the house. And while he was playing, two rabbits crept out from the bracken and peeped at him. One of them was brown all over, but the other had strange markings under his fur, as though long ago he had been spotted, and the spots still showed through. And about his little soft nose and his round black eyes there was something familiar, so that the Boy thought to himself:

"Why, he looks just like my old Bunny that was lost when I had scarlet fever!"

But he never knew that it really was his own Bunny, come back to look at the child who had first helped him to be Real.

Why can the Rabbit and the Boy be happy without each other?

"The one thing I fear most of all is a leak!"

THE TERRIBLE LEAK

Japanese folktale
as told by Yoshiko Uchida

One rainy night, long, long ago, a small boy sat with his grandmother and grandfather around a charcoal brazier. Warming their hands over the glowing coals, they told stories and talked of many things. Outside, the wind blew and the rain splattered on the thatched roof of the cottage.

The old man looked up at the ceiling saying, "I surely hope we don't have a leak. Nothing would be so terrible as to have to put up a new thatched roof now when we are so busy in the fields."

The little boy listened to the lonely
wail of the wind as it whipped through
the bamboo grove. He shivered and
turned to look at his grandfather's face.
It was calm and smiling and unafraid.

"Ojii-san," the little boy said suddenly.
"Is there anything you're afraid of?"

The old man laughed. "Why, of course,
lad," he said. "There are many things a
man fears in life."

"Well then," said the little boy, "what
are you *most* afraid of in all the world?"

The old man rubbed his bald head and
thought for a moment as he puffed on
his pipe.

"Let me see," he said. "Among human
beings, I think I fear a thief the most."

···

Now, at the very moment the old man was saying this, a thief had climbed onto the roof of the cowshed, hoping to steal one of the cows. He happened to hear what the old man said, and he thrust out his chest proudly.

"So!" he thought to himself. "I am the very thing the old man fears most in all the world!" And he laughed to think how frightened the old man and woman would be if they only knew a thief was in their yard this very minute.

"Ojii-san," the little boy went on. "Of all the animals in the world, which one are you most afraid of?"

Again, the old man thought for a moment, and then he said, "Of all the animals, I think I fear the wolf the most."

Just as the old man said this, a wolf was prowling around the cowshed, for he had come to see if there were some chickens he might steal. When he heard what the old man said, he laughed to himself. "Ah-ha!" he said. "So I am the animal the old man fears the most," and wiggling his nose, he sniffed haughtily.

But inside the house, the little boy went on. "Ojii-san," he said, "even more than a thief or a wolf, what are you the most, most, *most* afraid of?"

The old man sat thinking for a long while, and thoughts of ogres and demons and terrible dragons filled the little boy's head. But the old man was listening to

Why does the little boy want to know what his grandfather is "most, most, most afraid of"?

the rain as it splashed and trickled
in rivulets of water around the
house. He thought again how
terrible it would be to have a leak in
his roof. He turned to the boy and said,
"Well, the one thing I fear most of all
right now is a leak! And I'm afraid
one may come along any minute!"

Now when the thief and the wolf heard
this, they didn't know the old man was
talking about a leak in the roof.

"A leak," thought the thief. "What kind
of terrible animal could that be? If the
old man fears it more than a thief or a
wolf, it must be a fearsome thing!"

Down below, the wolf thought the
same thing. "A leak must be a dreadful
creature if the old man fears it more

than me or a thief," he thought. And he peered into the darkness, wondering if a leak might not spring out of the forest, for the old man had said one might come at any moment. Up on the roof of the cowshed, the thief got so excited he slipped and tumbled down into the darkness. But instead of falling to the ground, he fell right on the back of the wolf.

The wolf gave a frightened yelp. From somewhere above him in the dark night, something had leaped on his back and was clutching his neck. "This must be the terrible leak the old man talked about," thought the wolf, and with his tail between his legs, he ran pell-mell into the woods.

•••

Now the thief did not know he had
landed on the back of a wolf. He knew
he had fallen on the back of something
large and cold and full of fur. What's
more, it had given a wild yelp and begun
to run. The thief was so frightened he
couldn't even call for help. Instead,
he clung to the neck of this creature that
seemed to be flying through the night
into the forest.

"I must be on the back of the terrible
leak the old man talked about," he
thought fearfully, and closing his eyes
tight, he hung on. The harder the thief
clung to the wolf's neck, the faster
the wolf ran.

As they got deeper and deeper into the forest, branches of trees swung low and scratched the thief's face. Finally, when he felt a big branch sweep past, he caught it and swung himself up into a tree. But the wolf did not know what had happened, and he ran on and on until he came to his cave at the farthest end of the forest. When he finally stopped, he realized the thing on his back was gone.

"Ah, the leak has dropped off somewhere!" he thought, and he sighed a great sigh of relief.

Early the next morning, the wolf went to see his friend the tiger.

"Mr. Tiger, Mr. Tiger! What a terrible fright I

134

had last night," he said, panting at the very thought of it. "Do you know what kind of creature a leak is?"

The tiger shook his head. "Why, I don't believe I've ever heard of anything called a leak," he said. "What is it?"

"It is something human beings fear more than anything else in this world," said the wolf. "And do you know, one of those terrible creatures jumped on my back last night? I ran all night through the forest with this leak hanging onto my neck, for it clutched at me and almost choked me to death!"

The tiger grunted sympathetically. "Ah, how terrible that must have been," he said.

The wolf took a deep breath and went on.

"The leak dropped off somewhere after I got into the forest, but I'm sure it must still be here. If we don't capture it, none of us will ever be safe again. Will you help me to find it?"

The tiger nodded. "Certainly, I'll help," he said. "Besides, I'd like to see what a leak looks like. I wonder if it has two heads?"

And so the tiger and the wolf set off to look for the terrible leak. As they prowled through the forest, a monkey sitting in a tree peered through the leaves and saw them below.

"Say, Mr. Tiger! Mr. Wolf!" he called. "Where are you going with such worried frowns on your faces?"

"We are searching for a thing called a leak," they answered. "It is something so terrible that human beings fear it more than a thief or a wolf. It must surely be the most fearsome thing in the whole world, and we cannot live safely in this forest until we capture it."

The monkey listened carefully. "A leak?" he asked. "Why, I've never heard of such a creature. Surely, you must be mistaken."

But the wolf shook his head. "No, no! I am not mistaken, for this very creature clutched at my throat and rode on my back all the way into the forest last night. It dropped off somewhere and must be hiding near us this very minute!"

Now the monkey had seen the wolf running through the forest the night before, with the thief hanging on to his neck. He suddenly realized that this terrible thing they feared was only a human being, so he said in a loud, bragging voice, "Why, if that is the thing you are searching for, I can tell you where he is. He is sitting on one of the branches of the tree over there. In fact, I shall go and capture him single-handed if you want me to."

Why doesn't the monkey tell the wolf and the tiger that the terrible leak is only a human being?

137

The tiger and the wolf looked over at the tree where the monkey pointed. Sure enough, there, on one of the branches, sat a creature looking somewhat like a human being. The tiger growled and bared his long, sharp teeth. The wolf looked up at the sky and howled a long, piercing yowl. The thief heard their cries, and trembling with fear, he fell off the branch and went tumbling into a hole in the trunk of the tree.

As the three animals saw him fall, they ran over to the tree and stood around the hole where the thief was hiding.

"Now, how shall we go about capturing this leak?" they said to one another.

"Whoever captures him will become king of the forest," the tiger said. "For he will surely be the bravest and strongest of all."

"That is an excellent idea," said the
monkey. Then, because he knew this
leak was only a human being who was
frightened himself, he marched right up
to the hole in the tree trunk. He thrust his
tail inside and flipped it about, saying,
"Are you in there, Mr. Leak?
Are you inside?"

The thief had
heard the animals
as they talked
outside the tree.
"It will never do
to let them capture
me," he thought.
"For if they catch me,
they will surely kill me."

He decided he must do
something to frighten them
away, so he grabbed the monkey's
tail and pulled as hard as he could. Then,
he growled and shouted fiercely, trying
to sound more terrible than the tiger
and the wolf put together.

"Help!" shouted the monkey
as he felt his tail being pulled.
The thief pulled hard, but the
monkey pulled even harder,
for he didn't want to be dragged into
the hole in front of the tiger and the wolf.
They both pulled so hard the
monkey's tail broke off with a
snap, and the monkey went
sprawling onto the ground.
"My tail, my tail!
My beautiful tail!" he shrieked,
and he ran off into the forest,
disappearing into the leaves of
a tall cedar tree.
"The leak is certainly a
fearful thing," said the wolf, shaking his
head, and with a great howl he ran off
into the woods after the monkey.
"It is best to leave such fearful things
alone," said the tiger in a soft voice, and
he went slinking off into the woods
after the monkey and the wolf.

Why does the tiger decide that it is "best to leave such fearful things alone"?

•••

When all the animals had gone, the thief crept out of the tree trunk. He looked about carefully to make sure that nothing was following him, and then he ran as fast as he could out of the forest.

The thief never learned that what he thought was the terrible leak was only a frightened wolf. And the wolf never discovered that what he thought was the most terrible thing in all the world was only a frightened thief.

And the little boy and his grandmother and grandfather didn't have to be afraid of a leak in the roof after all, for in the stillness of the night the rain stopped, the moon came out bright and clear, and the next days were full of the promise of sunshine.

He heard music coming from among the trees.

The Singing Tortoise

West African folktale as told by
Harold Courlander and George Herzog

Far back in the country, near where the Adiri River comes out of the Kong Mountains, a hunter named Ama left his village one day to go hunting. Game was hard to find, and he went deeper and deeper into the forest looking for it. He came to the edge of the river in a part of the forest he had never seen before, and while he stood thinking where to go he heard music coming from among the trees. He heard a voice singing, and the faint tinkling of a *sansa,* which is a kind of tiny piano played with the thumbs.

The voice was singing:

"It is man who imposes
   himself upon things,
Not things which impose
   themselves upon man."

Ama moved forward quietly and
peered through the trees, and there,
sitting in a little clearing in the forest,
was a tortoise with a *sansa* in
her hands. She sang:

"It is man who imposes
   himself upon things,
Not things which impose
   themselves upon man."

Ama was astounded.
The tortoise sang beautifully.
Never had such a thing been heard
of in his country. He stood and listened.
The tortoise was not afraid but continued
to sing and play. The music was as
entrancing as anything Ama had
ever heard.

*Why does
Ama find the
tortoise's music
entrancing?*

144

He went back to his village after a while, but he couldn't forget the tortoise. The next time he went hunting in the forest he made his way again to the clearing, and there again he found the tortoise with her *sansa* and heard her sing:

"It is man who imposes
    himself upon things,
Not things which impose
    themselves upon man."

Every time that Ama was in the forest he went to hear the tortoise, for she was a strange and wonderful thing.

And then one day he thought how fine
it would be if he had the tortoise in his
house in the village, so that he could
hear her sing at night when he came
home from hunting or working his fields.
He spoke to the tortoise and asked her
if he might take her back with him.

"But this thing is a secret," the tortoise
said. "If you took me back with you
people would get to know about it."

"No," Ama said, "if I had you in my
house I would tell no one. It is only
I who would hear you."

"If that is true I'll go back with you," the tortoise said. "But I shall sing only for you, and the people of your village mustn't know."

"No," Ama said happily, "you shall sing just for me!"

He picked the tortoise up with great care so that he wouldn't hurt her, and carried her back to his house. And there each night when Ama came in from the fields or from the hunt the tortoise played her *sansa* and sang to him.

Yet it was such a wonderful thing that Ama couldn't keep from speaking about it to people in the village. He talked about it more and more. Among themselves the people ridiculed Ama for telling such a fantastic tale. No one really believed him. The story of Ama's singing tortoise spread farther and farther, and one day it reached the ears of the chief.

•••

"Who is this man who pretends to have a singing tortoise?" the chief said. "He will bring ridicule upon us with this silly story." And the chief sent messengers to Ama to tell him to come to his house.

When Ama came, the chief sat upon his stool in his courtyard, with his councilors standing by, and listened to the tale. Ama felt proud and important to own the thing that was causing so much excitement in the district.

Why does Ama feel "proud and important to own the thing that was causing so much excitement in the district"?

...

But the chief was disturbed, and the councilors shook their heads and were scornful of what Ama told them.

"There's no such thing as a singing tortoise," they said, "or a tortoise that can play a *sansa*."

"Everything I have told you is the way it happened," Ama said.

"You are impudent," the people said. "You are bringing disgrace upon us with your nonsensical talk."

Ama's feelings were hurt, and he said:
"I'll bring the tortoise here.
She will sing and play for you.
If she can't do this, then
you may beat me
for it!"

He went back to his village. Everyone was talking about Ama and his tortoise. He picked her up carefully and started off.

"Where are we going?" the tortoise asked.

"The people think I am lying," Ama said. "We'll show them!" The tortoise said nothing.

When Ama came to the chief's house there was a great crowd around it, for people had come from all the nearby villages to see what would happen. Ama placed the tortoise on the ground and put her *sansa* beside her.

"Now you will see," he said.

•••

The tortoise stayed quietly where Ama had placed her, and the people pushed close in a circle to see. But the tortoise didn't sing, nor did she pick up the *sansa*. The people waited. Nothing happened. The people argued among themselves. They became impatient. Minutes passed by. The tortoise pulled her head into her shell. Sometimes she put her head out to look at the people, and then she would pull it in again. Finally the people became angry.

"Well, when is she going to sing?" they asked.

"Sing for them so they will see I am not a liar," Ama said to the tortoise. But the tortoise only blinked her eyes. Time passed. People began to say angry things to Ama.

At last the chief said, "Well, we have seen. This man Ama has ridiculed us with his story. Now take him and beat him for it."

So the people took Ama where he stood and beat him hard with sticks. They beat him a long time, until the chief told them to stop.

•••

"This will teach you not to bring a bad name to our people by lying," the chief said. "Now pack your things and leave the village, for we have no room for such troublemakers."

Ama said nothing. His body ached and he was overcome with shame. He took his possessions and left the village. The people watched him until he was out of sight.

Why does Ama feel overcome with shame?

⸙

···

At this moment the tortoise put her head out of her shell and spoke. The people looked in wonder.

"Ama earned his shame through bad faith," the tortoise said. "He brought his punishment upon himself. I was happy in the forest singing and playing my *sansa*. Then he brought me to his house, promising to keep my secret. But he couldn't keep it. He told it to all the world, first in whispers, then with a loud voice."

Then she picked up her little *sansa* and sang once more:

"It is man who imposes
    himself upon things,
Not things which impose
    themselves upon man."

If three boys go all together it is not like always.

THREE BOYS WITH JUGS OF MOLASSES AND SECRET AMBITIONS

Carl Sandburg

In the Village of Liver-and-Onions, if *one* boy goes to the grocery for a jug of molasses it is just like always. And if *two* boys go to the grocery for a jug of molasses together it is just like always. But if *three* boys go to the grocery for a jug of molasses each and all together then it is not like always at all, at all.

Eeta Peeca Pie grew up
with wishes and wishes
working inside him. And for
every wish inside him he had
a freckle outside on his face.
Whenever he smiled the smile
ran way back into the far side
of his face and got lost in
the wishing freckles.

Meeny Miney grew up with
suspicions and suspicions working
inside him. And after a while
some of the suspicions got
fastened on his eyes and
some of the suspicions
got fastened on his
mouth. So when he
looked at other people
straight in the face
they used to say,
"Meeny Miney looks
so sad-like I wonder
if he'll get by."

...

Miney Mo was different.
He wasn't sad-like and
suspicious like Meeny Miney.
Nor was he full of wishes
inside and freckles outside
like Eeta Peeca Pie. He was
all mixed up inside with
wishes and suspicions.
So he had a few freckles and
a few suspicions on his face.
When he looked other people straight
in the face they used to say, "I don't
know whether to laugh or cry."

So here we have 'em, three boys
growing up with wishes, suspicions, and
mixed-up wishes and suspicions. They all
looked different from each other. Each
one, however, had a secret ambition. And
all three had the same secret ambition.

An ambition is a little creeper that
creeps and creeps in your heart night and
day, singing a little song, "Come and
find me, come and find me."

···

The secret ambition in the heart of Eeta Peeca Pie, Meeny Miney, and Miney Mo was an ambition to go railroading, to ride on railroad cars night and day, year after year. The whistles and the wheels of railroad trains were music to them.

Whenever the secret ambition crept in their hearts and made them too sad, so sad it was hard to live and stand for it, they would all three put their hands on each other's shoulder and sing the song of Joe. The chorus was like this:

Joe, Joe, broke his toe,
On the way to Mexico.
Came back, broke his back,
Sliding on the railroad track.

Why does singing the song about Joe help the boys when they are sad?

...

One fine summer morning all three mothers of all three boys gave each one a jug and said, "Go to the grocery and get a jug of molasses." All three got to the grocery at the same time. And all three went out of the door of the grocery together, each with a jug of molasses together and each with his secret ambition creeping around in his heart, all three together.

Two blocks from the grocery they stopped under a slippery elm tree. Eeta Peeca Pie was stretching his neck looking straight up into the slippery elm tree. He said it was always good for his freckles and it helped his wishes to stand under a slippery elm and look up.

While he was looking up his left
hand let go the jug handle of the jug of
molasses. And the jug went ka-flump,
ka-flumpety-flump down on the stone
sidewalk, cracked to pieces, and let
the molasses go running out over
the sidewalk.

If you have never seen it, let me tell you
molasses running out of a broken jug,
over a stone sidewalk under
a slippery elm tree,
looks peculiar and
mysterious.

Eeta Peeca Pie stepped into the
molasses with his bare feet. "It's a lotta
fun," he said. "It tickles all over." So
Meeny Miney and Miney Mo both stepped
into the molasses with their bare feet.

Then what happened just happened.
One got littler. Another got littler.
All three got littler.

"You look to me only big as a potato
bug," said Eeta Peeca Pie to Meeny Miney
and Miney Mo. "It's the same like you
look to us," said Meeny Miney and Miney
Mo to Eeta Peeca Pie. And then because
their secret ambition began to hurt them
they all stood with hands on each other's
shoulders and sang the Mexico Joe song.

*How does
singing the
Mexico Joe
song help the
boys here?*

···

Off the sidewalk they strolled, across a field of grass. They passed many houses of spiders and ants. In front of one house they saw Mrs. Spider over a tub washing clothes for
Mr. Spider.

"Why do you wear that frying pan on your head?" they asked her.

"In this country all ladies wear the frying pan on their head when they want a hat."

"But what if you want a hat when you are frying with the frying pan?" asked Eeta Peeca Pie.

"That never happens to any respectable lady in this country."

"Don't you never have no new style hats?" asked Meeny Miney.

"No, but we always have new style frying pans every spring and fall."

Hidden in the roots of a pink grass clump, they came to a city of twisted-nose spiders. On the main street was

a store with a show window full of pink parasols.

They walked in and said to the clerk, "We want to buy parasols."

"We don't sell parasols here," said the spider clerk.

"Well, lend us a parasol apiece," said all three.

"Gladly, most gladly," said the clerk.

"How do you do it?" asked Eeta.

"I don't have to," answered the spider clerk.

"How did it begin?"

"It never was otherwise."

...

"Don't you never get tired?"

"Every parasol is a joy."

"What do you do when the parasols are gone?"

"They always come back. These are the famous twisted-nose parasols made from the famous pink grass. You will lose them all, all three. Then they will all walk back to me here in this store on main street. I cannot sell you something I know you will surely lose. Neither can I ask you to pay, for something you will forget, somewhere sometime, and when you forget it, it will walk back here to me again. Look—look!"

As he said "Look," the door opened and five pink parasols came waltzing in and waltzed up into the show window.

"They always come back. Everybody forgets. Take your parasols and go. You will forget them and they will come back to me."

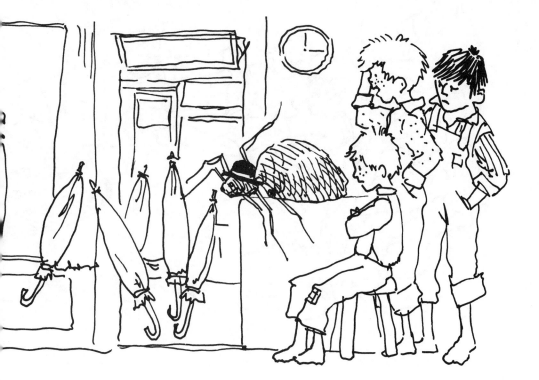

"He looks like he had wishes inside him," said Eeta Peeca Pie.

"He looks like he had suspicions," said Meeny Miney.

"He looks like he was all mixed up wishes and suspicions," said Miney Mo.

And once more because they all felt lonesome and their secret ambitions were creeping and eating, they put their hands on their shoulders and sang the Mexico Joe song.

How does singing the Mexico Joe song help the boys here?

ૐ

165

Then came
happiness. They entered the
Potato Bug Country. And they had luck
first of all the first hour they were in
the Potato Bug Country. They met
a Potato Bug millionaire.

"How are you a millionaire?" they
asked him.

"Because I got a million," he answered.

"A million what?"

"A million *fleems*."

"Who wants fleems?"

"You want fleems if you're going to
live here."

"Why so?"

"Because fleems is our money. In the
Potato Bug Country, if you got no fleems
you can't buy nothing nor anything.
But if you got a million fleems you're
a Potato Bug millionaire."

Then he surprised them.

"I like you because you got wishes
and freckles," he said to Eeta Peeca Pie,
filling the pockets of Eeta with fleems.

"And I like you because you got
suspicions and you're sad-like," he said
to Meeny Miney, filling Meeny Miney's
pockets full of fleems.

...

"And I like you because you got some
wishes and some suspicions and you look
mixed up," he said to Miney Mo, sticking
handfuls and handfuls of fleems into
the pockets of Miney Mo.

Wishes do come true. And suspicions
do come true. Here they had been
wishing all their lives, and had suspicions
of what was going to happen, and now
it all came true.

With their pockets filled with fleems
they rode on all the railroad trains of the
Potato Bug Country. They went to the

railroad stations and bought tickets for the fast trains and the slow trains and even the trains that back up and run backward instead of where they start to go.

On the dining cars of the railroads of the Potato Bug Country they ate wonder ham from the famous Potato Bug Pigs, eggs from the Potato Bug Hens, et cetera.

It seemed to them they stayed a long while in the Potato Bug Country, years and years. Yes, the time came when all their fleems were gone. Then whenever they wanted a railroad ride or something to eat or a place to sleep, they put their hands on each other's shoulders and sang the Mexico Joe song. In the Potato Bug Country they all said the Mexico Joe song was wonderful.

Why does everyone in the Potato Bug Country think the Mexico Joe song is wonderful?

·••

One morning while they were waiting to take an express train on the Early Ohio & Southwestern they sat near the roots of a big potato plant under the big green leaves. And far above them they saw a dim black cloud and they heard a shaking and a rustling and a spattering. They did not know it was a man of the Village of Liver-and-Onions. They did not know it was Mr. Sniggers putting paris green on the potato plants.

A big drop of paris green spattered down and fell onto the heads and shoulders of all three, Eeta Peeca Pie, Meeny Miney, and Miney Mo.

Then what happened just happened. They got bigger and bigger—one, two, three. And when they jumped up and ran out of the potato rows, Mr. Sniggers thought they were boys playing tricks.

When they got home to their mothers and told all about the jug of molasses breaking on the stone sidewalk under

the slippery elm tree, their mothers said
it was careless. The boys said it was lucky
because it helped them get their secret
ambitions.

And a secret ambition is a little creeper
that creeps and creeps in your heart night
and day, singing a little song, "Come and
find me, come and find me."

"Ah, how beautiful she is!"

CINDERELLA

Charles Perrault

Once upon a time there was a
nobleman who took as his second wife
the proudest and haughtiest woman
anyone had ever seen. This woman had
two daughters who were exactly like
herself in every way. The husband,
by his first wife, had one daughter,
whose gentleness and goodness were
unsurpassed. But this she had gotten
from her mother, who had been the
most admirable person in the world.

No sooner was the wedding over than the stepmother showed how mean she could be. She couldn't stand the excellent qualities of that young child, who made her own daughters seem all the more hateful. And so she gave her the worst chores in the house.

It was she who had to wash the dishes and scrub the stairs and clean the mistress's bedroom and the bedrooms of the young mistresses who were the stepmother's daughters. She slept in a garret at the very top of the house on a miserable mattress, while her sisters had rooms with parquet floors and beds in the very latest style and full-length mirrors.

The poor girl endured everything patiently. She didn't dare complain to her father because his wife ruled him completely and he would only have scolded her. When she had finished her chores she would go and sit among the cinders in the chimney corner, and for this reason she was known around the house as Cinderbottom. The younger daughter, who was not quite so coarse as her older sister, called her Cinderella. Yet Cinderella, with her miserable clothes, was nevertheless a hundred times more beautiful than her sisters, no matter how magnificently they might be dressed.

Now it came about that the king's son gave a ball, to which everyone of importance was asked to come. And our two young ladies were among those invited, because they cut quite a figure in the fashionable circles in that country. And so there they were, all aglow and all aflutter, choosing the outfits and the hairstyles that would be the most becoming to them—all of which meant more work for Cinderella, for it was she who ironed her sisters' linen collars and pleated their ruffles.

They talked of nothing but what they would wear. "I," said the older girl, "shall wear my red velvet with the English lace."

"Well," said the younger one. "I'm going to have a plain petticoat. But then I'll wear my overdress with the gold flowers and my diamond brooch. And there's nothing plain about that!"

They sent to the hairdresser to have double rows of horn-curls made up, and they ordered face patches from the patchmaker. Then they called in Cinderella to ask her opinion, because it was she who had good taste.

Cinderella gave them the best advice in the world and even offered to dress their hair, which they very much wanted her to do.

"Cinderella," they asked, as she was fixing their hair, "wouldn't you like to be going to the ball?"

"Oh, ladies! You're making fun of me. It wouldn't be proper for me to go."

Why does Cinderella say that it wouldn't be proper for her to go to the ball?

176

"You're right. People would laugh if they saw a cinderbottom heading for the ball." And anyone but Cinderella, hearing this, would have left their hair in a tangle. But she was so good-natured she coiffed them to perfection.

For nearly two days they went without eating, they were so excited. More than a dozen laces were broken, pulling in their stays to make their waists thinner, and they were constantly in front of the mirror.

At last the happy day arrived. Off they went, and Cinderella followed them with her eyes as long as possible. When she could no longer see them she began to cry.

Finding her all in tears, her godmother asked her what was the matter. "I wish . . . I wish"—she was crying so hard she couldn't finish. But her godmother, who was a fairy, said, "You wish you could go to the ball. Isn't that it?"

"Oh, yes," said Cinderella, sighing.

"Well," said her godmother, "will you be a good girl? I'll arrange it so that you can go." Then she took her to her room and said, "Run into the garden and bring me a pumpkin."

Cinderella went at once and got the nicest one she could find and brought it to her godmother, though she couldn't imagine how a pumpkin might get her to the ball. Her godmother hollowed it out, leaving only the rind. Then she tapped it with her wand, and the pumpkin turned into a beautiful coach all covered in gold.

Next she looked in her mousetrap and found six mice, all alive. She asked Cinderella to lift the door to the cage a little, and as the mice came out, one by one, she tapped them with her wand.

Each mouse was immediately changed into a beautiful horse, giving her a team of six horses in all, dappled a beautiful mouse gray.

She didn't know what to do for a coachman. Then Cinderella said, "Let me see if there isn't a rat in the rattrap. We could make a coachman out of that."

"You're right," said the godmother. "Go see." Cinderella brought her the rattrap, and in it were three huge rats. The fairy picked one of the three—on account of its superior whiskers—and as she touched it with her wand it was changed into a stout coachman with one of the finest moustaches ever seen.

Then she said, "Go to the garden. There you'll find six lizards behind the watering can. Bring them to me."

And no sooner had she brought them than the godmother turned them into six liveried footmen. They climbed right up on the back of the coach and stood there holding fast as though they had never done anything else in their lives.

•••

Then the fairy said to Cinderella, "Well, here's what you'll need to go to the ball. Don't you like it?"

"Yes, but am I to go in these ugly clothes?"

Her godmother simply touched her with her wand, and in that moment her dress was changed into a dress of gold-and-silver cloth all covered with precious stones. Then she gave her a pair of glass slippers, the prettiest in the world.

All dressed up, she climbed into the coach. But her godmother told her that above all things she must not stay past midnight, warning her that if she stayed at the ball a moment later her coach would become a pumpkin again, her horses mice, and her footmen lizards. And even her old clothes would reappear.

She promised her godmother that she would leave the ball before midnight, without fail. Then off she went, beside herself with joy.

Why does being able to go to the ball make Cinderella so happy?

When the king's son was told that a
great princess had arrived, whom nobody
knew, he rushed to meet her. He gave
her his hand as she got out
of the coach and led her
into the hall where the
guests were. There
was a great silence
then. The dancing
stopped, the violins
no longer played,
so intently did everyone
turn his attention upon the great charms
of this unknown person. The only
sound was a confused murmur of
"Ah, how beautiful she is!"

The king himself, old as he was, could
not help but gaze at her and whisper to
the queen that it had been a long time

since he had seen anyone so beautiful and so charming. All the ladies were intent upon studying her hair and her clothes, so as to have the same thing themselves the very next day, assuming that fine enough fabrics could be found and dressmakers with sufficient skill.

The king's son put her in the place of honor and then invited her to dance. She danced with such grace that people admired her all the more. A beautiful supper was served, but the young prince was so taken up with gazing at Cinderella that he could eat nothing at all.

She went and sat next to her sisters and showered them with kindness, sharing the oranges and lemons the prince had given her. At this they were amazed, because they didn't know her at all.

While they were chatting, Cinderella heard the clock strike a quarter to twelve.

She immediately made a deep curtsy to the assembled guests and left as quickly as she could.

When she got home she went and found her godmother, and after thanking her told her that she wished she could go to the ball again the next day, for the king's son had invited her. While she was telling her godmother everything that had happened at the ball, the two sisters knocked at the door. Cinderella went to let them in.

"How long you were!" she said, yawning and rubbing her eyes and stretching as if she had just woken up. Yet in fact she had had no thought of sleeping since they had last seen each other.

"If you had come to the ball," said one of her sisters, "you wouldn't have gotten so tired. The most beautiful princess came that anybody would ever hope to see, and she showered us with kindness. She gave us oranges and lemons!"

Cinderella
was beside
herself with joy
and asked
them the name
of this princess.
But they told
her that no one
knew, and that the
king's son was very upset about it and
would give anything in the world to know
who she was.

Cinderella smiled and said, "Was she
really that beautiful? Heavens, you're lucky!
Couldn't I see her? Oh, Miss Javotte, let me
borrow your yellow dress, the everyday
one."

"Really!" said Javotte. "Wouldn't *that*
be nice. Lend my dress to a repulsive
cinderbottom! I'd have to be mad."

Cinderella fully expected this refusal
and was just as glad to hear it, because she
wouldn't have known what to do if her
sister had actually lent her the dress.

*Why does
Cinderella ask
for a dress to
wear if she
knows her
stepsister will
refuse?*

The next day the two sisters went off to
the ball and so did Cinderella, dressed
even more elegantly than the first time.
The king's son was constantly at her side
and kept flattering her with soft words.

The young
lady found it by
no means tiresome. Forgetting her
godmother's warning, she heard the first
stroke of midnight while still thinking
it wasn't quite eleven. She arose and fled
away as lightly as a doe. The prince
chased after her, unable to catch her.
She dropped one of her glass slippers,

however, and the prince,
very carefully, picked it up.

Cinderella reached
home all out of breath,
without her coach,
without her footmen,
and in her miserable
clothes. Nothing was
left of all her magnificence except one
of her little slippers, the mate to the
one she had dropped.

The guards at the palace gate were
asked if they had seen a princess go by.
Only a girl in rags, they said, and more
like a peasant than a lady.

When her two sisters returned from the
ball, Cinderella asked them if they had
had a good time again and if the beautiful
lady had been there.

They said yes. But she had fled away at
the stroke of midnight, they said, and so
hurriedly that she had dropped one of her
little glass slippers, the prettiest thing in
the world. And the king's son had picked

•••

it up and had done nothing but gaze at it
for the rest of the ball. And no doubt he
was very much in love with the beautiful
owner of the little slipper.

What they said was true. Indeed, a few
days later the king's son had it proclaimed
to the sound of trumpets that he
would marry the girl whose foot
exactly fit the slipper.

It was tried first on
princesses, then
on duchesses,
and then on
all the court,
but without
success.

When it was brought to the house
where the two sisters lived, each in turn
did everything she could to make her foot
go into the slipper. But it was no use.

Cinderella was watching them,
and recognizing her slipper she said
laughingly, "I wonder if it wouldn't
fit me."

*Why does
Cinderella
pretend that
the slipper
might not fit
her?*

···

Her sisters burst out laughing and mocked her. But the nobleman who was conducting the test, having looked closely at Cinderella and finding her quite beautiful, said that this would be proper and that he had been commanded to try it on every young woman. He had Cinderella sit down. Then lifting the slipper to her little foot he saw that it went on without difficulty. It fit her as if poured on like wax.

The astonishment of the two sisters, great as it was, was even greater when Cinderella drew the other little slipper out of her pocket and put it on. Just then the godmother appeared and, touching her wand to Cinderella's dress, made it more magnificent than ever.

Her two sisters recognized her as the beautiful lady they had seen at the ball. They threw themselves at her feet, begging her to forgive them for all the harsh treatment they had caused her to suffer. Cinderella raised them up and

embraced them, telling them she
pardoned them with all her heart and
hoped they would always love her.

She was taken to the prince in her
magnificent clothes, and he found her
even more beautiful than before.
A few days later they were married.

Cinderella was as good as she was
beautiful. She had her two sisters come
and stay at the palace and arranged
for them to be married that same day
to two great lords of the court.

"Oh, that a son would fall down from the sky!"

THE MOUSE'S BRIDE

*Indian folktale
as told by Lucia Turnbull*

A farmer and his wife had no children . . . but one year, in the season of plowing, a strange thing happened to them.

Each evening as he came to the end of his day's work, the Farmer would lean on his plow and lament aloud, "My neighbors all have sons who will plow their fields when they are old and feeble. But I have none. What will become of my land? Oh, if I only had a son! Oh, that a son would fall down from the sky!"

···

One evening—when he was saying this
as usual—a hawk flew over his head,
and wondering, I suppose, to hear an old
man talking to himself, he spread his
claws in surprise, and out there dropped
a mouse . . . a little mouse, a boy-mouse.
And he fell at the feet of the Farmer.

The Farmer picked him up, saying,
"Where have you come from?"

"Out of the sky," replied the Mouse
simply.

"Will you come home with me?" asked
the Farmer.

"Yes, sir, if you like," agreed the Mouse.

"Will you learn to plow and sow and
reap?" continued the Farmer.

"My goodness, I can do that already!"
squeaked the Mouse, very much amused.

So the Farmer carried him home and
set him down on the table. But when the
Farmer's wife came in from the yard,
she gave a piercing shriek.

"Look, husband, look!" she cried,
clutching her sari around her. "Look,
there's a mouse on the table!"

"That is our son," explained the Farmer gravely.

"A mouse! Our son!" exclaimed the wife.

For a moment she thought her husband had been out in the sun too long and was raving.

"This little fellow dropped out of the sky," said the Farmer.

But the Mouse was very frightened. "Why is she shrieking?" he asked piteously.

"I do not know," replied the Farmer. "She was not expecting you—yes, that is it, she's taken by surprise. Enough!" he said to his wife and gave her a shake to steady her.

But now she was really looking at the Mouse, and suddenly she smiled.

"Why, husband, you are right," she said. "Yes, yes, it is our son."

195

Why does the Farmer's wife suddenly agree that the Mouse is their son?

And she hugged the boy-mouse
and gave him food, then put
him to bed. And in the
morning she made him a little
red coat, and he strode off into the
fields with his newly found father.

It was quite true what he had
said, that he could plow and sow
and reap. Very well he did it—some
days better than the Farmer himself.
Nothing could tire him. All day long he
worked, plowing late into the evening,
his paws clenched on the handles of the
plow, his face set in a frown, and his

whiskers gleaming red
with the setting sun.

Then the Farmer
would call to him,
"Come on, my dear,
come home. Look
how late it is."

The Mouse
looked up at
the sky, then

answered steadily, "I can still see to plow, Father."

"But look, all my neighbors' sons have gone home to supper," said the Farmer.

"Have they all gone?" The Mouse looked round as he spoke. "Are the fields quite empty?"

"There's Rama in the next field, just packing up," was the reply.

"I shall plow until he has gone." And the Mouse gripped the handles of the plow, to show that he meant what he said.

"Don't tire yourself, my son." The Farmer spoke kindly, for he had grown to love his adopted son very deeply.

"I am a strong mouse," said the little creature.

Not until the fields were empty would he stop work, and when he got home he would be merry and sing to please his parents.

The Farmer was so proud of him. He thought there was no better son on earth.

Why does the Farmer think there is no better son on earth than the Mouse?

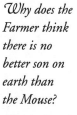

But after a time the little animal was no longer merry. He sang no more, and though he plowed as well and as long as ever, he was a different mouse when he came home at night.

Then the Farmer was grieved, but his wife—who knew other things than plowing—took a measure, and when the mouse was asleep, measured the length of his tail.

"Why are you doing that?" asked the Farmer.

"Hush!" replied the wife. "Hush, and I will tell you. Seven inches— exactly. What's three times seven, husband?"

The Farmer thought for a moment.

"Three sevens? Hmph! . . . three sevens are twenty-one."

The Farmer's wife gave a delighted nod.

"Yes, yes, I thought so!" she whispered.

"What did you think?" the Farmer whispered back.

"Our little boy-mouse has become a man," she replied softly.

"A man!" echoed the Farmer. "But why is he sad?"

His wife put the measure away.

"He is sad, husband, because he needs a wife," she said, and she looked tenderly at the sleeping mouse, who gave a tiny sigh as he snuggled in more cosily.

"If it's a wife he wants, I'll go and find him one," said the Farmer stoutly.

"Yes, tomorrow," agreed the woman. "But mind you, husband, she must be the best wife in the world to be worthy of our wonderful son."

The Farmer moved off towards the fire. "She must be like him, neither better nor worse," he grunted.

And so the very next day, the little man-mouse, in his red coat, and the Farmer, his adopted father, set out to look for a wife. And all day long they searched and found no one. As the sun set, they sat down on a stone. The Farmer was quite worn out, and even the Mouse was beginning to yawn.

Suddenly, the Moon stepped up into the sky, dazzling the Farmer with her beauty.

"Look, look, my son!" he cried. "There is a wife worthy of you. What do you think of her?"

The Mouse looked up at the Moon until he blinked. She was bright, she was radiant, but he did not much care for her.

So he turned to the Farmer and said, "True, she is very

beautiful, Father, but she
is so cold and proud."

"Yes, I am cold,"
scoffed the Moon.
"I am proud. I am
not for you."

The Farmer got
up and made a
deep salaam.
"Tell me, my Lady
Moon, is there none
better than you?"

"Oh, yes," replied the
Moon, "there is the Cloud.
When she covers me with her
mantle, I am invisible. She is better
than I."

At that moment a cloud slipped over
the Moon and hid her from sight.

"Look, look, my son!" said the Farmer.
"There is a wife worthy of you. What
do you think of her?"

"She is very fine," agreed the Mouse.
"But she's sad and gloomy."

"Yes, I am gloomy," mourned the Cloud. "I am not for you."

"Tell me, Lady Cloud," said the Farmer, "is there none better than you?"

"Oh, yes," replied the Cloud, "there is the Wind. She drives me all round the sky. She is better than I."

And at once the Wind blew hard and scattered the Cloud.

And now the Farmer thought he had found a fine wife for the Mouse and said, "The Wind now! She's just the one for you. What do you think of her?"

The Mouse shivered. "She sets my whiskers a-flutter, Father, but she fidgets so," he complained.

"Yes, I am restless," whistled the Wind. "I am not for you."

"Tell me, Lady Wind," said the Farmer, "is there none better than you?"

"The Mountain," replied the Wind promptly. "She is

far better than I. For although I storm, I cannot move her."

And the Farmer and the Mouse turned round and saw that they were sitting at the foot of a mighty mountain.

"There!" exclaimed the Farmer with relief. "At last we have found a wife worthy of you. Now then, what do you think of her?"

"She is very noble, Father, but I think she would be obstinate," replied the Mouse.

"Yes, I am obstinate," boomed the Mountain. "I am not for you."

"Alas, alas!" lamented the Farmer. "Alas, my son! It seems as if we shall never find you a wife! Tell me, Lady Mountain, is there none better than you?"

Then the Mountain groaned and said, "There is one far better, for though I am obstinate and do not budge, I know of one who will someday destroy me. Dig, dig into my heart. Dig deep!"

Then the Farmer took a spade, and the Mouse dug with his paws, and they made a hole in the Mountain, and were digging when the Mountain groaned again.

"Listen," she begged of them, "oh, listen! Do you not hear?"

And they listened.

"I hear nothing," said the Farmer.

"Set your ear to the ground," said the Mountain.

So they set their ears to the ground, and the Mouse's ear was the keener, it was so large and round.

"I hear a sound of scratching!" he cried in excitement.

The Farmer listened again.

"I hear it too!" he shouted. "Yes, it is most certainly something scratching."

"It is what I told you," sighed the
Mountain. "Dig on. It is in my heart."

So the Farmer dug, and the Mouse dug,
and the noise from the other side grew
louder . . . scratch, scratch, S-C-R-A-T-C-H!
And suddenly, the earth broke away
before them, and all they could see was
a gaping hole, black and deep, reaching
into the Mountain's heart.

Together they spoke in whispers
into the hole, "Come out, come out!
Come out, whoever you are!"

And there stepped forth from the
darkness a lady-mouse!

···

She wore a cloak of gray silk, her gloves were shell pink, and between her ears was a diadem of dewdrops. And the Farmer would have spoken—would have asked him how he liked her—but the man-mouse held up his paw.

"Do not speak," he said, as if under an enchantment. "This is the lady who must be my wife."

And he gave her his arm, and they walked home slowly together, the Farmer following, a light of wonder in his eyes.

When they reached home, the Farmer put his finger to his lips, and his wife nodded.

For she, you remember, knew other things than plowing.

Why does the Mouse seem to be under an enchantment after he sees the lady-mouse?

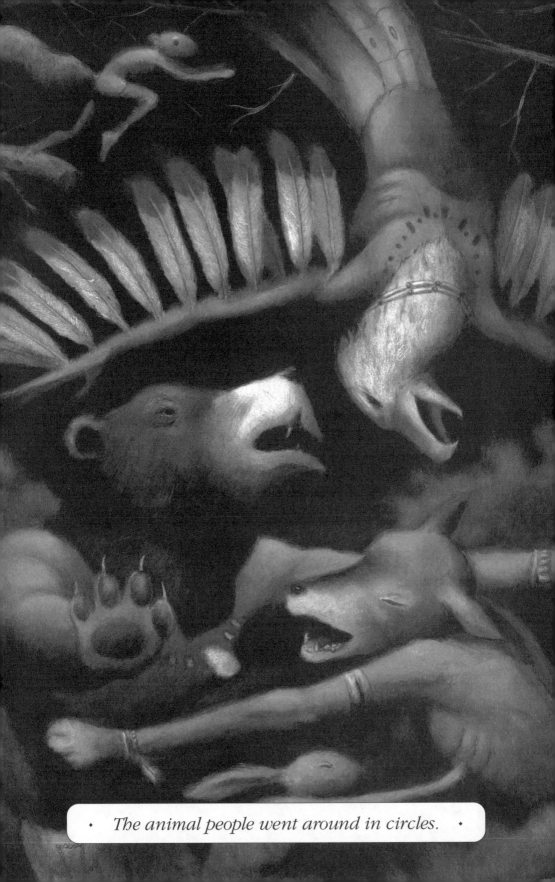

The animal people went around in circles.

How Coyote Stole the Sun

Native American folktale
as told by Jane Louise Curry

Back in the Beforetime, while the darkness Little Brother Weasel let loose still lay deep on the plain, every day was worse than the last. The animal people went around in circles. They bumped into each other and trees and their own houses. The bird people flew up and down, crashing into each other or the treetops or the ground. The darkness was so thick on the plain that it swallowed up even the light of the stars Little Brother Weasel had spilled from Roadrunner's bundle. And the darkness was full of the fog he had freed.

It was terrible. Fur and feathers grew damp. The ground grew cold. Teeth chattered. Beaks clattered. No one knew when to get up or go to sleep. The trees lost their leaves, and the grass withered. At first there was plenty to eat, for the oak trees dropped all their acorns, but only Wolf and Fox and Coyote, who had keen noses, had any luck at hunting. Even so, it was not long before they too grew lean and bony with hunger, for as they blundered about in the dark the deer could hear them coming, and the rabbits and mice kept to their holes.

"Tell us what to do," said the animal people of the plain to Sandhill Crane, their medicine man. "Tell us what to do," begged the animals who found their way to his house. "Tell us what to do," pleaded the folk who bumped into him in the dark. Crane could only sigh, for he had no answer.

Ki-yoo the Coyote grew angry. "If Crane does not know what to do," Coyote thought, "he should make something up. Something is better than nothing."

Why does Coyote get angry when Crane can't think of anything to do?

❧

···

And because something is better than nothing, Coyote ate up his last acorn, and trotted out into the darkness. There *must* be a better place for animal folk to live. And he, Coyote, would find it! He followed his nose to the river, the river to a creek, and the creek to a trickle of water that slid down from the foothills of the white-teepee mountain.

There, at the hill's foot, his nose caught a shimmer of a whiff of a sniff of the most delicious aroma he had ever smelled. It was nothing like the clear fresh tang of trout. It did not have the sharp, rich aroma of freshly killed venison. Yet even so, it brought to his mind mouthwatering visions of bounding deer and leaping fish.

So Coyote followed his nose.

As he trotted up into the Foothills Country he could think of nothing but the scent he followed. He did not notice the dim light ahead until after a while the darkness around him gave way to gloom.

Bare, shadowy trees appeared along the trail, and suddenly Coyote saw that he could see.

"Ha, hai! What can this mean?" thought he, and he trotted on all the faster.

Ahead, the light was brighter still. The trees wore leaves. The country began to be dry and warm. And the delicious smell was stronger than ever. When at last Coyote came near the place where the light was brightest, he spied the village of the Foothills People ahead.

...

Now, hungry Coyote might be, and brave, but he was cautious and cunning too. He sat and waited and watched. He waited until a fox, one of the Foothills People, left the village and came trotting down the path with his bow and quiver of arrows slung over his back.

"Hai, now we shall see!" thought Coyote.

In the twitch of a whisker he changed himself into a fox just like the other. The shadings on his fur, the notch in one ear torn in an old fight—all was the same. As Coyote-Fox trotted up the trail Fox had trotted down, he grinned. Not even Fox's mother could have told the difference between them, for Coyote's magic was strong. But, magic or no, the closer he came to the Foothills Village,

the lower Coyote's bushy tail
drooped and the harder he
panted in the heat of the
light in the sky above.

For the village had a Sun!

A Sun that hung from the
sky on a rope.

In the village not a head turned
as Coyote passed among the lodges.
When he stopped to drink from a
pitch-lined water basket, the pups and
kits nearby did not pause in their play.
One of the wives looked up from
stirring soup in a cooking basket by
the fire where cooking stones heated
and acorn cakes baked. But she turned
back to her work, and Coyote-Fox
trotted on to the next fire circle.

Cookfires! Coyote marveled. The
Foothills People had not only a Sun, but
cookfires! The wonderful aroma that had
drawn him through the darkness must
have come from the haunch of venison
roasting on the spit of the second fire.

Its fat sizzled and spat and dripped
onto the red coals. It smelled not at all
like raw venison. Coyote sniffed,
and shivered with pleasure. He touched
the meat and quickly licked the juice
from his paw. Hai, hee! It tasted as good
as it smelled. His empty stomach
rumbled as he turned away.

"I have seen what I came to see,"
Coyote told himself. "I must go before
Fox returns."

But then his stomach growled again,
as loudly as any grizzly. And he could not
bear to go. So he did not. He stayed,

sleeping in the shade,
until the chief of the
animal wives called
everyone to eat. Coyote-Fox
ate his fill of mush and fish and
roasted meat, and afterward slipped
away. Changing back into his own
shape, he turned his nose toward the
downhill path and hurried toward
the dark below.

Down in the dark, Coyote returned by
the way he had come. He followed his
nose to the trickle of water, and followed
the trickle to the creek to the river. But
between the riverbank and the village
on the plain he lost his way more than
once. When at last he reached home he
hurried to tell Crane of the wonderful
land where the animal folk had not
only a Sun and fire and good food, but
wives and pups and kits and chicks.

"It is truly wonderful," exclaimed
Coyote.

...

Crane was not so sure, for he was fearful of all things new. "The dark is bad, but this Sun sounds dangerous. It could burn our eyes and feathers and fur."

Coyote was alarmed. "Must we sit in the dark and starve, then? The hunters of the Foothills People have light to see and shoot by, and the wives bake acorn cakes and roast good meat. But we have no food to feed wives, and with no wives we have no pups or chicks."

Crane tossed his beak in pride. "We are strong. We have no need of what we do not have. If *you* must have them, then go back to your Foothills People."

Coyote went off and away in a huff.

"And so I will!" said he.

Once back in the foothills Coyote waited in the bushes by the village trail until he spied a bobcat coming out to hunt. Once the bobcat was past, he turned himself into just such a one. Bobcat's

wife could not have told the difference.
Brown-spotted coat, tufted ears—every
hair was the same.

In the village Coyote-Bobcat made
himself at home again. He ate the good
food. He watched the pups at play.
He admired the Sun. It was wonderful
even though it was very hot. And yet . . .

···

And yet, Coyote could not be happy. He could not forget his people in the flatlands. How could he be happy while they hungered and shivered down in the dismal dark?

There was nothing to do but go home again.

As soon as he reached his own village, Coyote sniffed Crane out and told him again how pleasant life in the Foothills Village was.

"And they take the Sun down at night so they can sleep. In the morning, if a cookfire has gone out, they poke a stick in the Sun to get fire to light it again. Then they hang the Sun up and have light to hunt and gather acorns by. A Sun is a wonderful thing. If we had one, you would like it. I know you would."

Crane rattled his feathers and hunched over against the cold. "Perhaps," said he, but still he was not sure.

"We could try to buy it," Coyote said eagerly.

...

"Not so fast, Ki-yoo!" Crane shifted
from one long leg to the other. "I know
you! You would bring this Sun here
with no thought how we could
make it work. How would
we hang it up? Our plain
is much farther from
the sky than the
foothills are."

...

"I will think of something," Coyote said, and he pestered Crane until at last, to be rid of him, Crane agreed that Coyote should ask the Foothills People how much shell money they would take for the Sun.

And so it was that Coyote went in his own skin to the Foothills Village to learn how much the Sun would cost. But the animal people there would name no price. Sell their Sun? Never! Not even a sliver of it. And they ran at Coyote and bit at his heels and chased him down into the foggy dark.

Why do the Foothills People refuse to sell even a sliver of the Sun?

•••

After the Foothills People turned back
to their village, Coyote sat on a log on
the border between the dusk and the
dark, and thought. They would not sell
the Sun. So he would have to steal it.
That would not be easy. The Sun was
kept at night in a house
made of sod with
no window
at all.

Its door was guarded by Turtle, Sun's
Keeper, and Turtle guarded it well.
He slept for no more than two or three
minutes at a time, and when he slept he
kept one eye open wide. It was said by
the Foothills People that at the fall of
a leaf on the roof near the smokehole,
or the pit-pat of the smallest foot
past the door, the Keeper of the Sun
would be up, with an arrow ready
to his bow.

...

How, Coyote puzzled, could he steal the Sun without stealing Turtle too?

At last he thought of a plan. He crept back up the trail and hid himself in a clump of bushes below the village. When the hunters came out again in the late afternoon to hunt, Turtle came too, gathering twigs and broken branches for firewood.

Quickly Coyote circled up and around. When he saw Turtle returning, he lay down across the top of the trail and turned himself into a large, crooked oak tree limb.

...

"Hai!" cried Turtle. "What luck! This will burn slowly and last all night." He set aside the pine boughs he had gathered and hoisted the heavy limb onto his back to carry it to Sun's house. There he dropped it atop the woodpile beside the fire circle and went to gather more before dinner. Coyote-Limb lay still. He was glad indeed that a tree limb could not feel hunger, for the smell of good meat roasting filled the house.

After the evening meal, the Sun was brought in for the night and put in a basket across the fire from Coyote-Limb. Turtle built up the fire, then picked up the limb and placed one end in the fire. But it would not stay. Because it was crooked, it would not lie flat.

"Limb, lie flat on the fire and burn!" scolded Turtle, but every time he pushed it down, up it turned again.

At last he lost his temper, lifted it up,
and dropped it—plop!—in a shower of
sparks across the fire. One end fell close
to the basket in which the Sun slept.

"Burn from the middle out, then!"
snapped Turtle. Turning away, he did
not see that, because of Coyote's magic,
the limb did not burn at all.

Coyote watched and waited until Turtle
settled down with one eye on the door.
"Sleep, Turtle," he sang under his breath.
"*Upija, upija*. Sleep, sleep."

Turtle's head drooped little by little until at last his chin rested on the floor. One eye closed and then, very slowly, the other. Soon Turtle began to snore.

Coyote-Limb tilted silently toward the Sun. Then, changing quickly back to his own shape, he hopped off the fire, popped a lid over the Sun, snatched up the basket, and dashed out and away.

Turtle awoke at once. "Hai!" he shouted out. "The Sun is gone! Someone has stolen the Sun!"

All of the Foothills People ran out into the night, crying, "Thief! Thief!" But they could not discover which way Coyote had gone, for he, coming from the land where all was night, was more sure-footed in the dark than they. While they bumped into each other and cried, "Thief! Thief!" Coyote bounded down through the foothills and into the darker dark below. When the cries of "Thief!" had died away behind him, Coyote lifted

the basket lid enough to light his way,
and trotted straight home, smiling to think
what a welcome he would have.

But it was not the welcome he looked
for. When the animal people of Coyote's
village saw the Sun they covered their eyes
and ran into their houses. They shouted
and scolded and would not come out until
Coyote covered it up again.

"It hurts our eyes!"

"Hai, how bright!"

"How are we to sleep with that shining through the thatch?"

"Take it away!"

Coyote took the basket to Crane, but Crane was afraid too, and would not take it.

"It was your idea," said Crane to Coyote. "*I* don't know what to do with it. We cannot hang it from the sky as your Foothills People do. If you wish to keep this Sun, Ki-yoo, you must think what to do with it."

Coyote went off in a huff. His friends were freezing in the damp and dark, and not a one of them had thanked him. Hai, ha! He would show them!

What does Coyote mean when he says that he will "show them"?

...

So Coyote slung Sun's basket on his back and traveled west to the place where the sky's edge meets the earth's edge. There, at the West Hole in the Sky, he took Sun out of his basket and ordered him to roll out through the hole and down under the World until he came to the East Hole in the Sky. When he arrived there, he was to come up and travel west, shining first on the Foothills People, and then on the plain. When he came again to the West Hole, he was to go under the world as before so the animal people could sleep. And every day he must do the same.

Because Coyote's magic was strong, Sun obeyed.

And when morning came and Sun rolled up across the sky, Crane and the others were glad at last. They could see where they were going. The days were warm. There was game to hunt. And all the trees and grasses grew again.

ACKNOWLEDGMENTS

All possible care has been taken to trace ownership and secure permission for each selection in this series. The Great Books Foundation wishes to thank the following authors, publishers, and representatives for permission to reprint copyrighted material:

The Other Side of the Hill, from THE SNOW PARLOR AND OTHER BEDTIME STORIES, by Elizabeth Coatsworth. Copyright 1971 by Elizabeth Coatsworth. Reprinted by permission of Grosset & Dunlap.

The Emperor's New Clothes, from IT'S PERFECTLY TRUE AND OTHER STORIES, by Hans Christian Andersen. Copyright 1938 by Paul Leyssac; renewed 1966 by Mary Rehan. Reprinted by permission of Harcourt Brace Jovanovich, Inc.

How the Elephant Became, from HOW THE WHALE BECAME AND OTHER STORIES, by Ted Hughes. Copyright 1963 by Ted Hughes. Reprinted by permission of Faber and Faber Limited.

Anansi's Fishing Expedition and *The Singing Tortoise,* from THE COW-TAIL SWITCH AND OTHER WEST AFRICAN STORIES, by Harold Courlander and George Herzog. Copyright 1947 by Henry Holt and Company, Inc. Copyright 1975 by Harold Courlander and George Herzog. Copyright 1986 by Harold Courlander. Reprinted by permission of Henry Holt and Company, Inc.

The Terrible Leak, from THE MAGIC LISTENING CAP: MORE FOLK TALES FROM JAPAN, by Yoshiko Uchida. Copyright 1955 by Yoshiko Uchida. Reprinted by permission of the author.

Three Boys with Jugs of Molasses and Secret Ambitions, from ROOTABAGA STORIES, by Carl Sandburg. Copyright 1922, 1923 by Harcourt Brace Jovanovich, Inc.; renewed 1950, 1951 by Carl Sandburg. Reprinted by permission of Harcourt Brace Jovanovich, Inc.

Cinderella, from THE GLASS SLIPPER: CHARLES PERRAULT'S TALES OF TIMES PAST, translated by John Bierhorst. Copyright 1981 by John Bierhorst. Reprinted by permission of Scholastic, Inc.

The Mouse's Bride, from FAIRY TALES OF INDIA, by Lucia Turnbull. Copyright 1959 by Frederick Muller Limited. Reprinted by permission of Century Hutchinson Publishing Group Limited.

How Coyote Stole the Sun, from BACK IN THE BEFORETIME: TALES OF THE CALIFORNIA INDIANS, by Jane Louise Curry. Copyright 1987 by Jane Louise Curry. Reprinted by permission of Margaret K. McElderry Books, an imprint of Macmillan Publishing Company.

ILLUSTRATION CREDITS

Brock Cole prepared the illustrations for *The Emperor's New Clothes* and *The Mouse's Bride.*

Diane Cole prepared the illustrations for *The Other Side of the Hill.*

David Cunningham prepared the illustrations for *The Red Balloon,* based on stills from the film of the same name, released in the United States in 1957.

Donna Diamond prepared the illustrations for *The Velveteen Rabbit.*

Ann Grifalconi prepared the illustrations for *The Singing Tortoise.*

Mary Jones prepared the illustrations for *Anansi's Fishing Expedition.*

Barbara McClintock prepared the illustrations for *How the Elephant Became.*

Emily Arnold McCully prepared the illustrations for *Three Boys with Jugs of Molasses and Secret Ambitions.*

Arthur Rackham's illustrations for *Cinderella* are from CINDERELLA, by C. S. Evans, first published in 1919 by William Heinemann.

David Shannon prepared the illustrations for *How Coyote Stole the Sun.*

Ed Young prepared the illustrations for *The Terrible Leak.*

Cover art by Ed Young. Copyright 1992 by Ed Young.

Text and cover design by William Seabright & Associates.